Evolution

Pathway to Embodiment

Evolution

Pathway to Embodiment

Anthony J. Rodriguez
~ Walking Crow

Dedication

This offering is dedicated to those who walk in the darkness and the light, but especially those who are eventually able to choose light.

To those who want better for themselves but have not known how to get to a place of healing.

To those who walk in darkness and have not found a way out, these pages offer *hope as does my heart…*

To my mother *Evangeline B. Rodriguez* and my father *David G. Rodriguez*, who brought me into this lifetime and who I had to learn to love deeply and without fault.

I love you mom and dad!

I would also like to honor the teachings of the mothers, grandmothers, great grandmothers, sisters, aunts, friends, and all the divine feminine and how they watched over me through my journey.

The teachings of the fathers, grandfathers, great grandfathers, brothers, uncles, and friends for the energy and light they bring in from the direction of the east.

Earth, Water, Fire, Air
Great Spirit and Mother Earth and all our Relations

A'ho Mitauiase!
With Gratitude, Love and Thanks,

Your Son ~ Walking Crow

Foreword

I first crossed paths with Anthony Rodriguez in the spring of 2015. I saw him speaking on Facebook Live, and something in his presence stood out to me. Not long after, he mentioned that he would be driving to Mt. Shasta. At the time, I was living in Ashland, Oregon, so I drove to meet him - never imagining that our connection would grow into a steady and meaningful friendship. It was a time when both of us were navigating challenging phases in our lives, and the meeting felt timely.

From early on, there was an ease in our conversations. He became a medicine brother - someone who simply understood, with whom I could communicate naturally. Ours is a connection that I share with only a few people in my life.

In 2017, I moved to Arizona to reconnect with my fiancé, Michael. Around the same time, Anthony also found his way to Arizona where his work and medicine deepened and expanded. We eventually both landed in Sedona, where I was able to work more closely with him - face to face, sharing ideas, projects, and perspectives.

Over the years, I have had the opportunity to walk beside him not only as a friend and collaborator - supporting his website, branding, and marketing - but also as a fellow elemental journeyer. He is someone with whom I can speak openly and directly. We have shared laughter, life experiences, frustrations, business discussions, meals, and many conversations about medicine and growth. Each exchange has carried a sense of mutual sharpening and encouragement.

There are very few people in my life I can say I truly know. Anthony is one of them. He is more than a teacher or storyteller, and he is more than simply a drum maker. He is the embodiment of Sacred Drum Medicine. His teachings and insights come from a place of authenticity and connection with Spirit. Observing the way he moves through the world - with grounded confidence, humor, honesty, and spiritual integrity - offers a clear picture of what it means to be guided by ancestral wisdom.

I have watched his evolution from Anthony to Walking Crow, witnessing a deepening in both his identity and his work. His presence carries both an ancient steadiness and a modern clarity - a combination that allows people to feel supported and genuinely seen. Walking Crow's approach is sincere and heartfelt, and he often speaks openly about choosing to embrace himself after a lifetime of challenges.

I have also seen many individuals go to him for support, only to discover that what he offers is not quick comfort, but true empowerment. He does not place himself above others; he walks alongside them. His medicine is lived, not performed - woven naturally into conversations, ceremonies, quiet moments, and every beat of his drum. His stories, lessons, and "medicine nuggets" are uniquely his. At times, his approach can be direct; he calls it "poking a bear with a stick," and often says, "If I'm rubbing you the wrong way, then I'm rubbing you the right way." And when I've had difficult moments, he has a way of breaking tension with a simple, lighthearted phrase like, "It's only Chuesday!" (or whatever day it happens to be).

Walking Crow brings a grounded lightness into heavy situations, offering perspective shaped by lived experience and delivered with genuine care.

To me, Anthony "Walking Crow" is a trusted friend and a steady reminder of what it looks like to live aligned with one's purpose. His teachings have impacted my path in meaningful ways, and his presence in my life has been a true gift.

This book is an extension of his work and his way of being. Within these pages, you will find not only insights, but an invitation to return to yourself, reconnect with Spirit, and remember the rhythm that lives within us all.

It is an honor to offer this foreword. May it be received with the same respect, clarity, and sincerity in which it was written.

Angela Jeanne Rose Heart
Rose Alchemy Healing
Vision Alliance Solutions
Sedona, Arizona

Preface

The road to embodiment was and is not always comfortable or easy, but as I became willing to say *YES* to the journey, the willingness grew within. I learned to say *YES* to overcoming fears, hurts, wounds, shame, and many years of trauma. By simply doing one thing to start, it was my *YES* that began to melt away a lifetime of pain.

The pain was not always recognizable, and neither was the truth or how to find the truth of what I didn't know how to feel inside. A life clouded by alcohol, drugs, food, sex, and obesity was transformed to a life of peace and happiness.

I am eternally grateful for the way the spirit world blanketed my soul and gave me a new vision for my future to share with others. Here between these pages lies the how and why of the embodiment that changed my life and the inner-standing I was given to just say *YES*.

Will you say *YES* after a lifetime of no? Can you say yes to me, or more importantly can you say yes to a transformation so powerful, you'll want to share it as I do?

Blessings and thank you to all that find their way to this offering of *"Evolution: Pathway to Embodiment."* May you be blessed and offer yourself the same hope I found in myself.

Just say *YES!*

~ *Walking Crow*
December 29, 2025
Sedona, Arizona

Acknowledgements

Thank you to all who believe because they can, for those who support with kind words, prayer, hope, tobacco, and smudge, and to those who gave me the "atta boy," that gave me more strength to believe in me and to believe in you. A special thanks to all who encourage and support my writing.

Aileen Lane
Alejandra (Alex) McAnderson-
   Villalobos (Mija)
Angela Jeanne Rose Heart
Bibiana Al-Rubaie
Brandon McAnderson Jr.
Brandon McAnderson Sr.
Carlos N. Iriarte
Cruz McAnderson
David G. Rodriguez (dad)
Deborah Haynes
Diane Sova
Dr. Gabor Mate
Dr. Theresa Smith
Eddie Hinsley
Julie Berstein
Maria Al-Rubaie
Martha & Frank Childres

Michele Matix
Rev. Emma Molina-Ynequez
Robert Lane
Robyn Quarles
Tony Smigiel
   (everyone wants to be a Tony)
Earth, Water, Fire, and Air
Great Mother
Layla's Bakery in Sedona
My Ancient Peoples
My family across Turtle Island
   and around the World
My Inner Knowing, Being, and Voice
Sedona and the Village of Oak Creek
Star Knowledge Peace Conference family
The Star Nations
The Universe and all it Encompasses

From my Heart, I thank you!
~ Walking Crow

Table of Contents

Introduction

In my early life, when confronted or choosing something new, I only did the things I actually understood or thought were cool or I could get something of value from, hoping others would be impressed by my unique style - which wasn't unique at all. I was living an ordinary life hoping to be discovered or recognized by some unseen force or entity. After all, I lived in Los Angeles where fame and prestige were just around the corner, or so it seemed. But for who?

I spent my young life moving from job to job starting at the age of eleven. I threw newspapers, sold sodas at park soccer games, then moved on to work in a liquor store stocking shelves and the cooler, sweeping the floors, and taking out the trash. As I got older my jobs changed. I went from working at places like McDonalds to working at Chief Auto Parts and freight shipping companies making more money hourly than most people, as the minimum wage then was about $1.98-$2.10 per hour. I worked hard and avoided trouble on the job, because there was none. No one was yelling at me, accusing me of misbehaving, or hitting me because they wore the uniform of the day and felt they had the right. Even if I was misbehaving, violence was not the answer.

I had no idea at the time, but everyday life was teaching me to be violent. Violence was justified through God, Jesus, the church, parenthood, and "because I said so." Educated in violence at home, school, God, and the world, no one ever took responsibility for the violence they created within the boy. When I acted out, I was a troublemaker (trabieso), a bad seed. As I grew older and wiser, I learned that *They were irresponsible with their responsibilities*, placing the responsibility on us (me).

Not being a good student and not believing I was very smart, I only muddled my way through school, seemingly getting into trouble at every turn. I knew at an early age what violence was because I grew up with it. I remember those late-night arguments between my mom and dad, when my mom defended herself from my drunken dad, who was mean when drinking. Much of the violence I experienced came from Catholic school and the people who were given charge over children, who mostly abused us and blamed us for their lack of ability and in the name of their so-called God.

At night I experienced the violence that came into my own home through television via the news channels. War, riots, protest marches where students were murdered by police, assassinations of political figures against those who marched for peace and stood for something good and righteous. Yeah. I was surrounded by it and was too young to escape it.

As I grew older, violence became less prevalent in my life, but the blame and anger directed at who I was remained - a constant slap in the face from parents, family, and teachers. It felt like the world was against me and that feeling only forced me to internalize anger, hate, fear, jealousy, and resentment. Feeling nobody cared, I didn't know that those younger years would haunt me through years of alcohol abuse, marijuana, drugs, stealing, food, sex, and occasionally violence.

But it wasn't all bad. Through childhood and into life, I developed a wickedly sarcastic sense of humor - one that got me into trouble as a boy but served me well once tempered by the wisdom I gained as an adult.

*Crowism:
"They were irresponsible with their responsibilities."
~ Walking Crow

Chapter 0: The Realization

Recounting the story of my being in the tree to an audience of one (my mom), who wasn't listening, I didn't give much thought to the fact that she wasn't listening. I know now it is more important that *I* was listening. I realized on the spot that the story was for me to remember and carry forward the medicine of the "tree of life." It wasn't enough for me to climb into the tree and sit in her branches from day to day. Eating her golden fruit and having that nectar course through my body and soul, the light began to shine within me. That lonely little boy got older and grew, totally unaware of the magic that was taking place within his darkness. I would have no idea of that light until a lifetime later.

As I began stepping into new roles, still not clear what those might be, people from all walks of life began to appear and I developed alliances with healers, teachers, masters, artists, musicians, psychics, astrologers, and beyond. A new world and pathways were opening up to me - when I paid attention and learned to allow it. I was once told to pay attention to signs and omens. I had no idea what signs and omens would look or feel like, but it wasn't long before I found out.

The sky seemed to take on a whole new way of being...or was that me seeing it with new eyes? Not my physical eyes, but the eyes within my heart. Not focusing on the obvious but seeing the passageways and portals that were becoming my new reality, I began to experience the wind as the force and the breath that also moved within my heart and lungs. It was no longer merely an external experience, but my internal reality of expanding my senses.

I met and began to work with a woman healer named Jeanne. My sessions with her were profound. We did clearings of the books of my life history and wounds I had been carrying. The sessions consisted of throwing those books into the fire and letting them go, releasing the heavy burdens. We traded sessions, and she came to my office where I cleared her with energy, giving her renewed balance.

We became dear friends through our continued sessions and she became one of my teachers.

Jeanne was also working with my wife at the time. We never went to sessions together and I never asked my wife about her sessions. As my abilities and sacred work grew stronger and I became more confident, Jeanne sometimes mentored me when I felt I was struggling. In fact, it was probably more often than when I was just struggling.

I remember driving to Palm Desert one time for an event with almost no money in my pocket. I was pounding on the steering wheel asking myself, "What am I doing?" I reached out to Jeanne on the phone and she responded with, "You asked for this life." I said, "I didn't ask for it, I said *YES* to it." I don't really know what the difference was either way, but I had made a choice and was willing to go forward with it, no matter what it looked or felt like in the moment.

As I moved forward in my walk, the relationship between my wife and I began to change. We grew distant and she at one time mentioned to me that she had a new teacher. Hmmm…I knew what that meant to her, as I knew her MO with regard to relationships. I was beginning to feel unwelcome as she was apparently spending more time with her new teacher. I knew who this person was but didn't feel it was my place to do anything. My life was changing and as upset as I felt, I knew it was part of what was meant to be. You see, we never know why others come into our lives until it is shown to us, and even then, it may not be quite clear. I learned much later that her gossip was that I was having an affair with my teacher Reverend Emma. That simply was not true. I respected Emma - she showed me trust and care and gave me guidance I had never received before.

As they worked together over time, my wife and Jeanne became closer and Jeanne and I became more distant. I never asked why, I just accepted that our relationship was over and our work was finished in that area. Now and again, I made efforts to reach out by telephone but never received a response or call back, so I just let go totally.

My wife and I eventually went through an uncomfortable divorce. I tried to be civil but had no capacity to do so. As a fifty-something year old, I had not matured in that way yet. I mean, I really wanted to and I tried, but there was still deep work to do moving forward to remove the blocks, wounds, and trauma that would lead to the opening of portals of light that have always been there. I just never knew how to access them until now.

My relationship with Emma deepened and we would meet for walks at the nearby Rose Bowl where the public went to walk, exercise, and gather for community events. Mike, her husband, would drive her and bring his bike to ride while Emma and I walked and talked. It was 3.5 miles around the Rose Bowl, so it was a good stretch of the legs. As we walked, Mike circled us, riding fast laps along the trail. Watching him brought us joy, and we yelled "heeeey" every time he sped past. The talks with Emma were deep and probing. She allowed me to talk freely and she listened deeply.

I began to notice a new kind of speech coming out of my mouth. I paid close attention, as I realized I was beginning to channel a new way of speaking with wisdom I had never given voice to before. Wisdom was not something I can say I was known for and honestly, I never felt I really had anything of consequence to say. I had always been a pretty shallow guy and everything I said to that point was ordinary and surface level.

Emma had slowly opened the door for me to blossom in a whole new way just by allowing me to speak and allowing me to hear myself for the first time in my life. She nurtured the part of me that had never known that kind of nurturing and care. I had never been truly listened to or asked for my opinion. I was always blurting out stuff to be funny, to be noticed, and to get attention - sometimes inappropriately.

I had long been starving for attention, having felt ignored and rejected in my earlier years. With Emma, though, it was different. She gave me the space to expand my thoughts and offered guidance I believe only she could provide, helping to shape my words and the new wisdom that began to emerge through them. With Emma I felt loved and cared for, as well as with Mike. He spoke simple, kind words to me and even hugged me from time to time.

Emma began calling me Mijo, which means son in Spanish. I took pride in hearing her call me that. My mother, of course, would call me that too, but it felt different. Not that my mom was mean or angry, but as my spiritual relationship with Emma grew and was nurtured, the meaning felt different and warm in a new way. I felt like I finally had someone in my corner and there was something special about that for me deep inside.

It's a funny thing going through life not knowing that I was missing anything. I mean, what did I know? This might seem odd to hear, but *"I only knew what I knew."* You don't know until you know and I was beginning to know, ya know? Lol.

I began to laugh at myself as well. I mean, I laughed at myself before, but it was an uncomfortable kind of embarrassed laugh. What was I embarrassed about? I was embarrassed that I felt dumb and ignorant, that I didn't know anything, and you might notice or find out. But all that began to change as I developed my spiritual muscle, doing pushups on a daily basis to move further and further away from those feelings of unworthiness. I don't know if I could have done this without the friendship, help, love, and support from Emma. I mean, I have no reason to believe otherwise. Everyone could use an Emma in their life!

When we spoke on the phone, texted, or saw each other, Emma called me Crow, but when she called me Crow it sounded and felt different than when anyone else did. I could feel the Mijo in her voice as she called out "Hi Crow!" It was her tone that meant something.

There was pride in it, love, care, and inner-standing. I beamed from the inside out which I had never done before.

Even at my mom's house, when I walked in and my mother greeted me with "Hey Crow!" I giggled inside and felt the warmth of her meaning, giving her a hug and kiss before settling in for a visit. I have to say, when my mother called me Crow there was some sarcasm involved and a little bit of her making fun of it, as I don't believe she understood the Crow thing. I didn't expect her or anybody else to understand the changes or new acceptance I was stepping into. I just listened to her greeting and received it in my own way.

My insides began to react less and less to the words and behavior of others as I started to understand that they (others) are none of my business and the things about them were not about me. There is a place in the Bible where Jesus talks of being about his father's business. That's how I felt. I was going inward and that was my soul purpose and journey. So I began to listen in a new and maybe even in a compassionate way.

Compassion really started to come in after an experience I had with a friend who was a healing client. I was conducting an energy healing and as the session went on, I noticed someone standing in the room on the other side of the massage table at my client's feet. The figure wasn't doing anything, just standing there. I checked in with my eyes to see if I was imagining things, but nope, there she was. She was a strange being, obviously female and Asian, wearing a long gown or robe that I think was either light powder blue, soft yellow, or off white. I know these colors are all different, but as I write, it was years ago and I just remember the color to be soft. She wore a strange hat and radiated a gentle, peaceful presence.

The healing session ended and afterwards I asked my client if he had seen or experienced anything unusual. I told him about what I had seen, but he had no memory of it. He asked, "Is there something I should know?" and I responded, "I don't know." I knew I had to investigate and search out what or who I had seen. I told him I would let him know once I found out who our visitor was.

As I sat with my experience, I heard the words "Ascended Master." So off I went to a metaphysical bookstore not far from me and found a book on the Ascended Masters. I could have thumbed through the book to find what I was looking for, put it back on the shelf, and leave, but I didn't. I purchased the book, took it home, and sat quietly with the contents between the covers until I came to a familiar figure with the name of "Quan Yin," also known as "Guanyin" and "Kuan Yin." She is revered in East Asian Buddhism, especially China, and is widely regarded as an ascended Master of compassion and mercy. Also known as a Bodhisattva, she embodies the qualities of loving-kindness and compassion and protector of those who are in need.

Interestingly, my client, who is also a close friend of mine, worked as a defense attorney. When I learned the meaning of Quan Yin, I reached out to him to talk about the power of compassion as a guiding virtue. More than anything, I shared how leading with a compassionate voice can open the way to a more compassionate heart. Hearing these words come out of my mouth, I understood they were not just for him, but for me to hear and take into my voice and heart to become compassionate with myself first. After mastering this for myself, I would share and have greater compassion for others.

I believe that charity starts at home and learned in Alcoholics Anonymous that I couldn't give away what I haven't got. So I became my greatest love - as uncomfortable as that could be for a guy like me. My hard walls and sarcasm began to melt within, and I developed the ability to just BE and nothing else. I no longer had to be what you wanted me to be or what I thought others wanted me to be. I no longer had anything to prove to myself or anybody else. In theory this seems easy and maybe it is, but my reality is that my memories bubbled up and I began to doubt and fight myself. I found that this was just a byproduct of transformation and change. It began to fade as I practiced and did the pushups necessary to strengthen the muscle of a healthier spirit.

Compassion is a funny thing when you've never known it. At first, I began to pick and choose what I was actually going to have compassion for, being I had no experience. Whether it was for myself or others, it was a slow journey. It is said that "slow and steady wins the race," so I took this to heart and treated myself with kid gloves moving forward, always remembering that I am only spirit made flesh and my flesh or humanness will have its moments. I remember my Alcoholic Anonymous sponsor David saying to me "Hello human," as I was having meltdowns in early sobriety, then laughing at myself and my ridiculousness.

"Truth will make us wince and if the shoe fits..."
~ Walking Crow

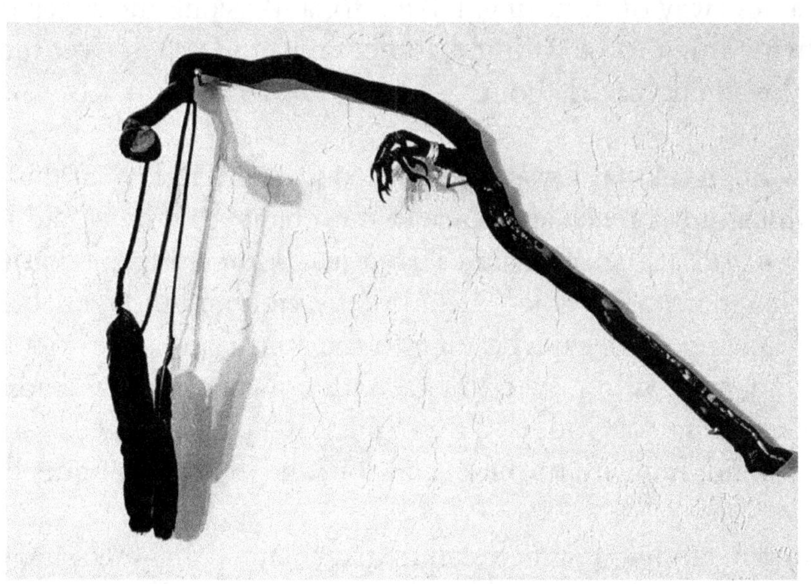

Walking Crow Talking Stick

Chapter 1: Untying the Knot

Making my journey while traveling the Red Road, I began venturing out on my own to unfamiliar places in the Los Angeles area. I set out on long hikes in the canyons and pathways in the local San Gabriel Mountains. This is something I had never done before I began to change my life, always staying within the safe confines of my suburban city life, where I felt at home and familiar. Or so I thought. The more I walked the trails of the canyons, the more comfortable I became in the wilderness - and in my own body and mind.

During this time, I was attending sweat lodge in San Fernando, the town of my birth which I thought was interesting. I was taught by my elders that when you are in the ceremony of sweat lodge you are re-entering the womb of Mother Earth. Before I entered, I was to ask permission. I took this seriously. I could feel my body changing as I began connecting with Mother Earth and the spirit world. I began to speak and understand from a different place. It also changed the way I behaved and approached nature when I was hiking and exploring. I found a new way of honoring, talking to, and asking the ancestors in every living thing to be with me, to help me, and watch over me and those I loved and cared about.

My view of a god that I was conditioned to fear and love at the same time, which didn't make any sense to me, changed. Why would I love and fear a god at the same time? That just sounded like a confusing and broken narrative to me. The more my view and thoughts of God began to change, I began speaking to the spirits and ancestors living all around me, within everything. With my new understanding, I started referring to God as Great Spirit, which resonated not only with my mind, but with my heart and soul and every part of my being.

From understanding to inner-standing, it changed my walks and hikes as I connected with plants by touching, feeling, smelling, and tasting as I passed. Finding different kinds of sages growing in the wilderness, I picked some to take home with me and used those to cleanse and clear the energies in and around me.

I learned that we do not just take from nature without asking or offering something in return.

I felt that prayer wasn't enough of an offering, so I began to purchase and carry tobacco with me all the time, using it when asking permission of Mother Earth. As I began to harvest the sage medicines more and more, I was led to different places where it grew and only took what I needed. Doing this, I never had reason to purchase it in a store, because Mother Earth always provided what I needed.

There were many lessons in all the things I did. The more I gathered sage medicines, the more excited the child in me became, as he reconnected with and grew alongside the adult me. I began gifting sage to people I knew, also part of my transformation. Then I began offering it for sale, until I learned through my elders and their teachings that this was not our way. I immediately stopped selling it and chose instead to offer it only as a gift. From then on, I always carried it in my car. Whenever someone said they needed to buy some, I simply said, "Hold on," went to my car, and returned with the plant medicine in hand. Many offered payment, but as I said no to taking their money, I realized I was saying *YES* more and more to Mother Earth and the spirit world.

By stepping into feeling and letting go of the need to think my way through what I was doing, how I was behaving, and how I was living, I began loosening a juggernaut that would eventually come undone, releasing the lifelong grip it had held on me. I moved into my heart and did things for different reasons. I may not have known at the time, but spirit eventually gave me a new way of knowing, doing, and being.

I began to see, feel, and speak differently, discovering a new voice. I started speaking a language of the heart and spoke boldly, releasing all fear of what others might say or think about the transformation unfolding within me. My voice found a new power of fearlessness and certainty, unafraid to stand up and be seen. Don't get me wrong,

Creator Great Spirit didn't just snap its fingers and poof, I was different. Nope!

The information and new way of speaking came with great struggle, as I had always been told I was dumb, which made me feel worthless. I constantly doubted myself. My world had mirrored those things to me and I swallowed those beliefs hook, line, and sinker. Regardless of the internal struggle, I moved forward with a new inner-standing of my true SELF. My inner child became stronger and willing to step forward to eventually integrate fully with my inner man. After a lifetime of feeling worthless and unloved, living in the emptiness of the "hole," I became "whole." That hole hovered just over my sternum or third chakra, the place of low or no self-esteem, the place of fire which wasn't burning very bright.

As I gained trust in the spirit world, I was able to go back and rescue my inner little boy from that lost place, showing him love he had never been given, and merge him with the man after a lifetime of separation. Unwinding a tangled soul is not for the weak or for the carefree, it's deep dark hard work and most of the time just unbearably uncomfortable. I believe that through my willingness to remain open and to trust, I was able to find my path forward.

When deciding to change the narrative that caused years of hurt and suffering, you have to know there will be collateral damage, if I can call it that. People from my younger life began falling away and I felt no reason or obligation to reach out or explain. I kept walking and those that inner-stood understood! The only person I owed anything to was myself and my inner little boy who was now becoming whole in an accelerated way.

There were days I felt extreme loneliness and wanted to reach out and ask for help, but very little help was to be found. I certainly didn't find any through my marriages and relationships. I didn't feel like I could go to my elders to talk about it, either. I probably could have, but I wasn't called to. Isolation and stillness were the order of the day.

When I experienced those feelings of deep loneliness, I was being taught to sit with myself and to be still with the emotion (I call it emocean).

At the time, I didn't understand and my perceived loneliness became bearable over months and years. My willingness to listen into the silence became primary, and I sat quietly more and more until it became a daily occurrence when I rose every morning. I began not using an alarm clock to wake up in the morning unless I was going to travel. Not using an alarm, I began to let my internal clock work on its own, to wake up organically when my body and soul were ready.

Some days I woke at 7:00 a.m. and some days it was 9:00 a.m. As I began working for myself and the greater community, I was able to shape my schedule in ways that cultivated a more peaceful rhythm and released the sense of urgency the world had taught me - which was to give everything, and I mean *everything*. I began the practice of sitting quietly, sometimes for an hour, sometimes for 3-4 hours. The urgency of 'have-to' slowly melted away from my way of life. As I nurtured my new path and way of being, I experienced complete silence for the first time and floated in it.

In the film *Amadeus*, Wolfgang Amadeus Mozart composed concertos only to be disappointed when his performances were canceled after just two or three shows - often due to the King's reaction, or the perceived reaction shaped by jealous officials who resented Mozart's extraordinary talent. When Mozart met with Antonio Salieri, who was the King's core composer, looking for answers and compassion for his work, Antonio complimented him, then told him that "Mozart makes too many demands on the ear."

This phrase always stayed with me as I am a fan of Mozart. Making too many demands on the ear is what the world does to the soul, mind, and spirit. Unlike Mozart, the world oversteps its bounds to oppress us with ridiculous demands of "Do this and do that," "Don't do this and don't do that," leaving us in confusion and unable to connect to our higher self. The world diminishes our spirits via alcohol, drugs, food, sex, depression, disease, and a myriad of life challenging problems.

I no longer choose the shoulds or have-tos - the poisons the material world offers, which once hypnotized me. Freedom is mine, and it can be yours, too, if you want it. All I had to do was reach inward and allow myself to let my life - not theirs - unfold. I allowed the juggernaut to unravel itself, not cutting the cord, but let the unraveling happen organically through my growth and the embodiment of my own spirit.

Evolving into the "being of the doing and the doing of the being" is the way I have chosen to embody with grace and dignity. It is what I call a "Crowism," one of many that have been downloaded from spirit. I now speak from my renewed core values, never feeling like I have to apologize for what I say or who I am. I excused and apologized for myself throughout my life to make others feel better but in the process making myself small. Standing in my roots, my grounded nature, I am able to carry my voice and body forward, healing along the way while no longer apologizing for anything…*anything*!

Taking a stance like this is a powerful thing after a lifetime of apologizing for nothing and never being able to have my own voice. The voice that came out of me was the voice of others - of society, the colonizer's voice, television, and the lies it spilled all over me. The lies of obedience, submission, and "Do as I say not as I do."

When I finally returned to the moment my inner little boy splintered off, I brought him forward and merged him with the man I was, becoming "whole" after a lifetime of "hole." When I say hole, I'm talking about the emptiness I lived with. Becoming whole, I was finally able to crawl out from beneath the rock that had unknowingly weighed me down for a lifetime. At the time, I had no awareness of what was - or wasn't -happening to my soul. But as I grew spiritually, moving from darkness toward light, it became unmistakably clear that something had been off for most of my life. As I began to feel and understand this truth, I found myself wanting more and more of this new flavor of life.

This was something I had never experienced before, and I found myself fully immersed in the essence and wholeness of my new life. Understand that saying *YES* is a powerful gesture and action for me. Just as importantly, saying no to the patterns of a lifetime is empowering but often threatening for some people.

An audience is always present, even though you may not have noticed yet. Not because all eyes are fixed on you, but when your voice changes - when the mannerisms and behaviors that once carried you through life begin to shift - it becomes clear that something has happened. Those who notice have their eyes opened by your new way of being.

Many will not like what they see or feel, because the mirror is now unavoidable. What was once ignored or left unacknowledged is suddenly exposed and reflected back to them.

Am I bothering you?

> *"If I'm rubbing you the wrong way I'm rubbing you the right way."*
> ~ *Walking Crow*

Wow! How powerful is the truth of your *YES*? Mine has the power of transmutation, transcendence, and transformation. The ride of the transition is often beyond the words of description. The fire that burns inside of me after years of cold ash and fire without spark was reignited by a simple *YES* that apparently wasn't so simple, the willingness to give myself more than I ever felt I deserved or was led to believe by a vicious world and again, by those who meant well but had no ability to give me better.

I gave myself permission to breathe into my body after a lifetime of breathing without purpose. My new purpose was shown to me through suffering as I ascended - rooted and fruited - into a powerful tree, my branches reaching outward to the world around me and upward to the heavens. In that ascent, I came to understand the depth of what I had to offer a world that had been waiting patiently for me to rise. She never turned her back on me; she simply waited patiently for my *YES* - for my willingness to grow from the roots of my foundation to bear fruit in abundance. In that knowing, I understood I would never be without.

What majesty! How majestic I have become, willing to see myself in a magnificent light. Understand this: the beauty of a lotus does not suddenly appear one day out of nowhere. No! It grows slowly over a lifetime, gradually ascending through muddy darkness and the murky waters of "emocean" (emotion), making its way toward a light that has been shining on its waters for eons. When it finally reaches full ascension, then - and only then - do I fully become the Lotus, piercing the light in my fullness and brilliance as the flower that I am and have always been.

Never giving up on myself, no matter how murky those waters of emocean became, I stepped into my place in the sunlight, my spirit visible to all, embracing the "I am" I was finally willing to see, become, and accept as my own.

Once you begin the ascension and truly feel the power of living a purposeful life, there is no turning back to doubt, apprehension, self-pity, self-hate, or self-loathing. All those things begin to melt away, and with renewed purpose a new journey unfolds - one step at a time - toward a happiness one could not have known or imagined until now.

Oyae shi no? Oyae shi no? Oyae shi no? Oyae shi no?
Are you ready? Are you ready? Are you ready? Are you ready?
~ Walking Crow

Chapter 2: Standing in the Dark

As much as I was willing to stand squarely in the center, taking my place in the sunlight of my spirit through the power of my *YES*, I have no doubt about how deeply the darkness served me. Like the mud surrounding the lotus, it held me, guiding me toward hope even though I wasn't able to understand it at the time. I am always reminded that without darkness there is no light and without light there is no darkness. It wasn't until I stepped onto the path of becoming a healer, guided by my own healing, that I began to glimpse how little I had truly understood the world around me.

Darkness is something that many humans don't understand, because they rely on their physical eyes to determine whether something exists or does not. Their beliefs tell them what *is* or *isn't* - yet most of those beliefs do not come from within. No! They come from the outer world: mother, father, programming, government, schooling, religion, television, newspapers, and movies that assume authority to keep us in fear for their own purposes. I believe their purposes are rooted in control, money, and the maintenance of a false power they have convinced people to accept as real.

Truly, the agenda of institutions like Catholicism, government, and big business are the things they don't want you to know about, shrouded in lies, deception, and manufactured truths. All of it cloaked - you guessed it - in darkness! They know this darkness all too well and try to disguise it as light. What those invested in the illusion fail to reckon with is that true light illuminates and draws attention to precisely what they are trying to hide. It is said the greatest trick or lie is convincing people that evil doesn't exist, even when it's right in front of them.

The devil, evil monsters, people of darker skin, and the unknown have long been associated with darkness, as if always holding the possibility of something terrible happening. You hear this echoed in the voices of people, reinforced by governments, and amplified through so-called entertainment. What we don't understand, we fear and because we don't truly understand darkness, we give it labels that distort and misrepresent its reality.

I grew up as a case of the fear of darkness. I was told as a child by my father that my mother didn't love me because I was darker than the rest of the kids. I didn't understand it at the time, but that set a precedent for the rest of my life and how I moved through it. Fear, embarrassment, shame, ugliness, and a feeling of not being wanted hung in my mind, body, and soul for what felt like a lifetime.

As a child everything feels like forever, so when I say lifetime, I guess I mean lifetime as a child, which is forever. I lived and grew up one block from the railroad tracks, behind the Foothill Division of the Los Angeles Police Department in Pacoima, a lower middle-class neighborhood full of Mexican, Italian, Irish, Polish, and Japanese Americans. Ours was a neighborhood of true diversity that was quiet except for the train and police sirens. We never had any problems with neighbors. In fact, the neighborhood was so safe everybody left their doors unlocked or open when they went to the store or ran errands. You hear this kind of thing about neighborhoods across the country. But nowadays, you can't do that in the Pacoima I came from.

Across the tracks on Hanson Hill and Lake View Terrace is where the African Americans lived. As kids we would ride our bikes or walk across the tracks to play at the local parks or go to Muscatello's Bakery. It was during the time when race was an issue in other parts of the country, when neighborhoods were burning in places like Watts and Chicago, but there was little or no difference between the folks in my neighborhood. I mean, everybody was friendly and spent lots of time speaking over back fences.

But I was darker than the rest of the kids. Not just those in my family, but amongst the kids on the block as well. I was short, husky, and funny looking with crooked teeth, and no sports talent whatsoever. I was always the last one picked for teams, if I was picked at all. I'm not saying I was never picked for games, but there were always faces and comments made when doing so. I loved the battle when I was picked. Like when I got a hit when playing baseball on the street or making a shot while playing basketball or horse was the greatest feeling I could ever have. Catching a baseball in a game was just as amazing, because my biggest fear was not catching the ball and having to hear ridicule from the other guys. That kind of nervousness ran through my body and was with me for years. Looking back there was a lot that I carried that a kid shouldn't have to.

The same neighborhood kids and I would cross the tracks to explore the washes and underground tunnels that were pitch black. Without fear, we would explore them for what seems like hours, walking in water and darkness. Even doing things like this, we never encountered trouble and as scary as the dark was, we did it anyways. After all, we were a group and we looked out for each other. I believe that if our parents knew where we were, we probably would have gotten a talking to or an ass whooping, lol! But we didn't worry about that, we were having fun.

As I stepped into my healing and emotional transformation, I began to remember the not-so-pleasant experiences of the darkness in my life. The things I drank, drugged, and ate to escape. The darkness that didn't show itself outwardly or that others could identify. Those things lived so deep inside that I pushed them down further with alcohol, drugs, pot, food, sex, anger, and humor. Those were the things that I acted up over, the crux of my anger, things I tried to cover up with humor as I got older. I believed I got funnier and funnier, with things coming out of my mouth until they became inappropriate in classrooms and elsewhere in the outer world. These are the things that got me in trouble and the reason I was labeled as problematic and a troublemaker. I became the kid with a bad reputation. I was the problem and I was to blame and they let me know it.

What a discomfort I felt through my body as those things made themselves apparent in my life. I was never proud of the things I suffered through. I say suffer because I had no skills to deal with the hurt and the hurt was deep. I'm grateful they all didn't bubble up at the same time. That would have been so painful I can't say for certain if my mind, body, and soul would have survived it. I mean the chances of me being here to write and witness for others to read and understand would have been slim to none. There's a piece of truth that couldn't stick in my throat.

I have to tell the story from when I was a young boy about things bubbling up in time.

When I was a boy, my father and I would arrive home on Sunday after a long day at the park watching the soccer matches, with my alcoholic father drinking throughout. On the way home, dad would stop to buy a six pack of some beer and/or a bottle of whisky, with me allowed to get Milk duds and a small bottle of Seven Up. Dad drove, swerving his truck across the lanes of traffic trying to navigate us home. Those short rides were really long and scary journeys. Those are memories that have not and will not ever be forgotten.

I mean, it doesn't rule my life, but when I recount the story, it sits in the forefront of my mind, saying *here I am, tell me, tell them, let them know.* We always made our way home in time to get ready for dinner. I would sit with my treasure of Milk Duds and Seven Up, opening the box and dumping the Milk Dudes onto the table, then twisting the lid off my Seven Up to take care of the business at hand before dinner. I would put those Milk Duds in my mouth one at a time, slowly letting the chocolate melt before chewing the caramel center. The Seven Up in its green seven-ounce bottle sat in front of me waiting. I could hear the gas from within the bottle hissing as I sat chewing my deliciousness. Wow! Those things I loved as a boy, pure sweetness.

I would stare at the shiny green bottle of Seven Up as I chewed, watching bubbles form on the bottom of the bottle. Every now and again a bubble would release and float to the top and pop. I had no idea at the time why that caught so much of my attention, but as I walked through the releases into transformation as an adult, it reminded me of this time in my life as memories came up or bubbled up one at a time. There is much significance in the memories from my past life as a child that were very important in the transformation of the man. It's like transporting back and forth through dimensions and time.

Darkness is not always bad or evil. I learned early on in my sobriety that there was nothing in the darkness that wasn't there in the light. I was always afraid of the dark as a child. My mom would tell me to take the trash out at night, and this feeling would immediately come up in my gut and mind. Fear was instant and I had no idea why. I went outside into the darkness and walked towards the trash cans and as I made that short walk, I always looked around for whatever would pop out of the darkness. I would toss the trash into the can, turn, and run back to the safety of the house. I don't know exactly what I was afraid of or what could possibly have been in the darkness that wasn't there in the light.

As a younger boy, when we played outside at night in the dark I didn't have those scary feelings or fears. We played hide and seek and I hid in dark places so as to not be found. When did that shift to fear happen in me? Why did I become afraid of the nothingness and the possibilities of what could be there in the dark?

After I got sober, I decided to test myself. One night, I went into my room with the lights on and stood in the middle, looking around at my surroundings. Then I walked over to the light switch, turned it off, took a few steps back to the center of the room, and stood waiting for something to happen. Nothing! Nothing happened or came out of the dark. I walked back over to the switch, flipped it on, and took my place back in the middle of the room, looking around to see what had moved or what was different. Again, nothing! Nothing had come out of the dark to move or change anything. My feelings and fear of the darkness around me and within me changed from that point forward. I had never told anybody or expressed my fear of the dark. That was a deep secret between me and darkness.

I stepped into my present state of being as a healer, accepting my role of Transformational Sacred Drum Medicine and allowing it to take root within me. As I embodied this path, I recognized myself as earth, water, fire, and air - the living elements of Mother Earth. I understood that I was both earth and spirit, and I leaned into that knowing, steeping myself in belief in who I was becoming while remembering who I had been. True transformation was unfolding, and despite moments of doubt, I accepted my place.

As I began to talk my walk and walk my talk, more and more teachings from the darkness were coming to me and through me. I began to have a new inner-standing (understanding) that the darkness was a part of me, not separate from me. I inner-stood that I was sun and moon, earth and sky, fire and water. I stopped running and hiding from myself and the true nature of what was always me.

My mind was transmuting and I started living in my heart and doing everything from that place. This was not easy as I began to speak of it and those around me tried to correct my voice and talked as if they didn't understand. But no matter, I understood and kept walking and talking as the medicines within me flourished and grew. I grew. Wow! What revelations I was having! I began to speak in a way that only I could and was gifted transformative words by the spirit world that I stood by and repeated as truth. I understood that there is no evolution without revolution and revelation. I steamrolled forward and unearthed, uncovered, discovered, and embraced the darkest parts of me as well as the brightest light that shined through me.

I uncovered the reason I was afraid of the dark for so many years as I more and more said *YES* to my transformation and evolution through revolution. The reason was a direct result of my willingness to look and go deeper into the darkness. I realized I had to return, in real time, to rescue the little five-year-old Tony, who was waiting patiently for me to rescue him from the darkness that had held him for a lifetime. When I appeared in front of him, he stood and raised his arms, wanting to be picked up by the man who had left him behind, splintered by trauma.

I picked him up, held him in my arms, and repeated the Ho'oponopono prayer to him over and over, asking for forgiveness for not being able to take him with me as I grew up. I also forgave him for not being able to come with me. I held him and rocked as we cried together, forgiving each other quietly. This began the long road of integration of the boy and the man, so we could eventually become whole after a lifetime of hole and emptiness.

The shadow work was what I needed to understand my 'whys' and all the reasons my inner little boy was left behind over and over again. Doing the deep work in those dark spaces meant I had to look at things I avoided for a lifetime, honestly come to terms with them, and find answers and healing in the steppingstones forward. That meant I had to look into the mouth of the lion and return home to the place and space of my birth.

I obviously had no awareness of my body and soul when I was born into this world. But as I grew, my experiences with my parents and between my parents eventually revealed a lot. It wasn't apparent in my early years but as I began to run and play on the school playground, it was obvious at times that something wasn't well with me. I never mentioned it to anyone, especially my parents, but as I played with the other kids, I would get an expanding feeling - a burning in my chest - and became short of breath. This only happened when my activity level peaked, like when I tried to run full speed. I would have to stop and force myself to breathe slowly to even get a deep breath. My breathing was shallow and labored, my chest burning with each inhalation. It would pass and I would forget about it entirely - until the next time it happened.

Eventually, these episodes subsided and I even thought they went away. But in my adult life, when I became a private trainer and an aerobics instructor, it reappeared. Teaching choreography at the highest level for forty-five minutes at a time, I would have to stop myself during the workout while my students went on with the routine. Again, I would find myself bent over with my chest burning, trying to slow and catch my breath. I didn't understand and honestly, really didn't try to figure it out.

It wasn't until years later, after I left my fitness training behind and got sober, that I finally brought this issue to my doctors' attention. By this time, I had developed allergies to plants, grasses, smoke, and who knows what else. Along with an inhaler and allergy meds, the doctor prescribed diabetes and blood pressure medicine. I was not accustomed to taking aspirin much less prescription meds.

Healing my shadow and its wounds, spirit revealed that the issues in my tissues originated with the abuse my mother suffered while I was in the darkness of the womb, perpetrated by my father's darkness in his drunken and alcoholic states. I understand that she felt unloved and her heart was broken. I also understand that this energy landed in my lungs. By this time, I had learned the physiology of energetics on the emotional body and how it affected me all my life.

To understand was to say out loud, "Heart lungs air, I'm loved, I love" or "Heart lungs air, I don't have the lung capacity to love, and I don't have the capacity to be loved." This is where the true broken state of my emotional body was revealed, a clear and important understanding. I began clearing my body of the trauma, both mine and my mother's, and began to heal. I never had to use an inhaler again or take allergy meds. I had healed my heart space, loving myself to wholeness. I love and I am loved by my inner-standing.

Understanding these things allowed me to heal. I began sharing my journey with others, revealing that they could have the opportunity to begin their own healing by saying *YES* to themselves after a lifetime of no. As I became willing to share more of my journey, it was obvious my light was beginning to shine through the darkness. I became a beacon, a lighthouse for guiding others on a path of safety for their own healing. I always remind people that I can't and won't do it for them, I am simply a wayshower.

I found comfort within the darkness as all fear left me. I allowed my light to shine and loved the light I was becoming and am at this very moment. I stand in my brilliance and understand I walk and talk in illumination. Whether you choose to see me or not, I see me and feel me - that is the only thing that matters.

> *"I gave the darkness a chance.*
> *It took me in its embrace as I illuminated from within."*
> ~ Walking Crow

Dreamcatcher

Chapter 3: Opening to Other Worlds

As I grew into the man I was becoming, other worlds opened up to me. What other worlds, you might ask, and what does that mean? They are the unseen and unfelt realms we often miss because of our conditioning, our programming, our distractions, and the absorption of false teaching and information we take in throughout our lifetime. That includes distorted, fake American history spoon fed to us through schools and media. Propaganda is one such world I want nothing to do with. I refuse to fall prey again to those who profit from feeding on the fears of the people. I believe this is how Madison Avenue, big pharma, big business, and government institutions thrive, playing on fears of not having enough, not being enough, and wanting more.

Moving into the spirit world allowed me to free myself from the beliefs that kept me trapped and in bondage for a lifetime or even lifetimes. I had swallowed the lies hook, line, and sinker, adopting a belief system that was never truly mine.

Many people become part of 'movements' not from deep personal conviction, but from low or no self-esteem. They become joiners, devout listeners to what I call the common rhetoric of the common parrot, who simply repeat what they've been taught, unsure how to claim a thought, feeling, or voice of their own. They want to be different from the pack, but like the hippie movement of the 60s, they end up just being different together, never realizing they've been programmed like the rest.

This was how I lived my earlier life - amongst the lies and hypnotic zombiism of others. I often say, "The parrot parrots the parrot that parrots the parrot of the parroting parrot," that people or social zombies believe as truth. I lived in those lies and even got in line and spouted those things as truths. I became a joiner and believed that I was somehow special or different, even though I looked, talked, and did as others did. I didn't want to be singled out as I had been singled out my entire life for what I felt were all the wrong reasons. I wasn't special or different at all; I was plain wrap just like the rest. I watched the same television, listened to the same radio, wore the same clothes, and made efforts to fit in everywhere under the confusing guide of being a peacock. Lol! Looking back, I have to laugh at the fool I was and probably still can be at times, even as I move forward in my transformation and the releasing or shedding of the old self.

The world of anger, sadness, hurt, want, need, and desperation consumed me, but there was never any reason to believe anything was wrong - because everyone around me was the same way. Like covering myself with a blanket in 100° heat, it was uncomfortable, but we were all there. So I drank and drugged like everybody else, hung out putting myself in potentially dangerous situations, and got involved in the dangerous world of drug dealing - because the money seemed to be good, I thought I was cool, and I was always surrounded by hangers-on.

Those were the worlds I was willing to leave as I stayed sober through Alcoholics Anonymous, another world in itself. It was a world where everybody walked, talked, and acted the same way, but with a purpose. Their purpose was not to drink. I did everything possible so I could become and stay free of my alcoholic nature - which I nurtured one sip, drink, or gulp at a time. I found myself there through the court system and decided to stay as I really had nowhere else to go. Walking and talking like a duck seemed to be good for me when it came to getting and staying sober, seemingly becoming free from the lash of my own self-destruction.

Seemingly!

I say *seemingly* because I had carried so much inside for years, hiding it from the world - or so I thought. Lol, seemingly! Learning to laugh at myself became part of the program. My sponsor, who helped me maintain my sobriety day by day, had a way of asking questions or making provocative remarks that forced me to stop and think things through - or at least slow me down when my thinking spun out of control. Much of that confusion and inability to understand myself or the world came from my low or non-existent self-esteem, which was the real reason I drank in the first place.

Choosing to attend a ceremonial sweat lodge opened a world I had missed for most of my life, tethered as I was to the material world. Sitting in the lodge with ceremony taught me to return to humility, to the earth, to soil and dirt, to Mother Earth herself. I later came to understand that this return was the source of my strength, my breath, and my life. It taught me to ask for permission before doing anything.

When crawling into the lodge, I bowed with my face to the ground, asking Mother Earth for permission to enter, only doing so after I had been smudged with the sacred medicine of sage. There were protocols to adhere to and I learned them quickly. Until then, I had never truly belonged to anything other than church and Alcoholics Anonymous. Here, my elders taught and shared the protocols of the ceremonies I was stepping into. For me, this was life-changing, soul-changing, and world-changing as I attended monthly and did as I was taught.

Stepping into the world of spirituality and stepping onto the way of the Red Road became the driving force of my life. I learned to sit still, listening and noticing what unfolded in the darkness surrounding me. For four or five hours, the outer world fell away, and nothing was as important as being present with Mother Earth, Great Spirit, the fire, the rocks, and the lodge, along with the spirits that gathered around me within the safety and sacredness of the ceremony.

I learned to sit in the searing heat as steam rose off the rocks when water was poured over them. Slowly, I found my place within my own skin and accepted this community of elders and men, who welcomed and accepted me. We shared fellowship, prayers, and a meal each time we emerged from the lodge, as if being birthed from the womb once again.

My heart, mind, and soul were illuminated as I moved through the darkness of returning, and I began to see the women in my life differently. They became sacred, special, and worthy of reverence - especially my mother, as it was through her body and womb that I entered this life. I recognized that I had been wasting those gifts, waiting for women like my mother and other expressions of the divine feminine to serve me. I could finally see how wrong I had been for so long. The call to honor and serve them was strong and I began to shift, serving women with respect, humility, and care.

This was not easy, I have to admit. I had no healthy role models for how men should act in relationships with women. I had never seen the men in my life interact with their partners in loving and respectful roles. The only example I saw was how my father treated my mother. I set out on my own, connecting more and more with Mother Earth each time I crawled into her womb.

In my relationships, what seemed to be falling apart was actually the inner man coming together. I released and finally accepted the wounded child within me, along with the childish ways I had used to survive. I transformed into a new way of being. I had been acting out and mistreating women for so long that it felt normal. But it wasn't. It isn't. And that was changing. My heart softened and opened, and I felt myself rebirthed with a new love for myself and for the divine feminine - who had always deserved my love, admiration, and respect.

Rev. Emma, along with her daughter Victoria, came into my life during this time and we became fast friends. More than that, we became what I call a soul family. Emma and I used to meet and share meals along with deep conversations, including the deep listening that I had become attuned to in ceremony. We walked and took long hikes as Emma lent her ear and heart to me, sharing my intimate nature. She never judged me or made me feel bad for my thoughts or feelings, always listened attentively, and offered sage responses when necessary. This was a comfort as I had never experienced this, either with my wives or social companions. Her daughter Victoria took me under her wing as well, spending quality time with me. I felt they were molding me into a new man - and quite frankly they did, along with the help of the spirit world.

One day, Victoria invited me to her home to birth a dreamcatcher. I didn't know how to do this, but I said *YES* and showed up, carrying a long branch that I had in my possession for months. I had picked it up on one of my many hikes in the foothills of the Los Angeles or Pasadena area. While the stick was still wet, I had created a hoop with it, tied with the thinnest parts of the end of the branch like rope or twine. Over time it had dried, and this is what I used to birth the dreamcatcher. Sitting with Victoria in this process was illuminating for me. I listened to her direction as she patiently showed me and walked me through the birthing exercise of the creation of the dreamcatcher. She taught me the ins and outs of weaving together the thread, and within a couple of hours my dreamcatcher was finished for the time being. If you were to ask me to teach you how to weave a dreamcatcher, I would honestly have to tell you that I don't know. I believe my lesson was sitting in the stillness of listening and being with Victoria for a bigger experience to serve me in my future.

These women took the time and gave me care, love, and listening while holding me in a light I had never been held in before. I learned to love for new reasons, right reasons that had nothing to do with taking, getting, or disrespecting others. It was simple kindness, which I carry with me today because it showed me what it feels like to truly receive and be nurtured by others.

I was also learning how to navigate relationships with the men in my life. Not all men, but those who found me worth their time like my friend Carlos. He was a busy young man who still made space to share and listen deeply. I began noticing that friendships among men often stay at the surface level. We have conversations about everyday things like what's happening at home or with our wives and children, but somehow deeper feelings are usually bypassed. We aren't accustomed to having those kinds of conversations. I'm not saying that is true for all, but it's the truth for many. By watching and listening to others, I learned how much goes unspoken due to fear of judgement or lack of understanding. I also learned that not everyone cares, and that what feels deeply important to me may not matter to them at all.

I've been married three times. Each one of my wives was culturally different, which meant they were raised differently than I was. My first wife was white, raised in Tennessee. My second wife was from Bogotá, Colombia and my third wife was Hawaiian and Basque. Three very different women, each with her own history, culture, and way of being, reminding me that being American is not a single experience. I am of Mexican descent, although still American, very differently raised. Just because we know a person who lives next door doesn't mean we know or understand how they are as people or where they come from.

I believe I didn't have the ability to understand my relationships because I wasn't raised within a healthy relationship. I wanted to love each of my wives but had no real understanding of how to do that, rooted in the lack of a meaningful relationship with my mother. Understanding that, I have to admit I had even less of a relationship with my father. His alcoholism created a deep barrier between us, even though I came from his seed and lived in his house.

I attended the schools they sent me to, which added more to my feelings of disconnection. I remember my father asking me again and again when I was in trouble, *"What are they teaching you in school?"* Really? There was no responsibility taken by him - and I will say by my mother either - as they turned me over to people who had the same issues we did and were even more irresponsible with the children in their care.

So I nurtured the relationship with Carlos and I called him friend. Through many conversations, we began to understand where each other came from. Carlos had made a success of himself as an attorney.

I was still trying to figure everything out at well over fifty years of age. But here we were developing a meaningful friendship.

This was the beginning of many important and trustworthy relationships, something I had never truly experienced before. The connections I had assumed to be meaningful were always tied to something else like drinking, drugs, women, sports, or whatever superficial thing came next. All those relationships were temporary and none lasted more than a few years.

When I first discovered sweat lodge, I invited Carlos to attend with me. I hadn't experienced ceremony yet and honestly didn't want to do it alone. He said yes and we met for lunch midday before heading off to something neither of us fully understood - yet.

Arriving at the property, we were greeted by an elder who was kind and welcoming. I was asked not to come empty handed, but to bring tobacco as an offering, a monetary donation, water to share, and food to share after sweat lodge was finished, as we would celebrate our rebirth coming out of the womb. I thought I was doing a good thing by inviting Carlos, but the elder who greeted us took me aside and admonished me for bringing him. It's not that Carlos wasn't welcomed. The elder told me that they wanted to know those who would attend. Point taken, I apologized to my elder and to Carlos for my indiscretion I wouldn't make that mistake again. These were new relationships and for me navigating the unknown, it was important to feel like I was doing the right thing. But I often asked myself, "What is the right thing?"

This began the journey towards taking responsibility for my actions, my inactions, and becoming the man I was always meant to be.

Closing the door on my old world and stepping into the new was exciting. Everything felt fresh and parts of me were slowly being reborn. But I didn't shut out the past completely. I left the door cracked, allowing myself to move in and out of those old feelings so

I could finally make peace and become whole with them. I had been splintered by those experiences for a lifetime, and it was time for wholeness in my life by becoming a friend to myself. It wasn't just about having new friends; it was about learning how I could truly *be* a friend.

This was a world I could and wanted to live in comfortably, to be a friend as a friend. To listen, give time, caring, maintaining intimate relations that had nothing to do with romance, only the desire for closeness and true fellowship.

The early friendships in my life were left behind as I grew and moved forward. I never felt the need to go back and reignite old times. They simply weren't that important to me. I believe that if they had been, they would have evolved with me. I just wasn't wired to hold on that way, and even now I can't fully explain why. What I do know is that I don't want to chase friendships that aren't present or willing. I believe relationships require two to work. Before, I exhausted myself trying to keep up with notes and phone calls that felt unwanted or ignored. Reciprocity is a practice of want and willingness. If I felt others were not willing to make the investment in a relationship, I just let go.

Even now, when someone doesn't or won't respond, I stop investing my time and energy. It isn't a waste of time until it becomes a waste of time, know what I mean? Over time, people telling me how much they love me and appreciate me started falling on deaf ears when they weren't matched with actions. I came to understand my own value and if all someone could offer was lip service, I was willing to give up any more effort.

I've always believed "you can't talk out of both sides of your mouth at the same time." Lip service, double talk, empty promises, and the dangling carrots became unappreciated and unwanted in my life or in my heart. My intuitive nature had evolved so much that I could sense and feel it when someone wasn't being truthful, even as they spoke.

I came to understand this as my Owl medicine, the gift of listening and feeling, of seeing truth and presence in the darkness. I had been belittled for much of my early life and knew what that behavior sounded, felt, and looked like. I understand that some people are so broken and hungry for validation they will say just about anything to garner badly wanted attention, even if just for a minute or two. Their words are empty, with no truth behind the words expressed.

When someone is not willing to go inside and take the deep dive of a thorough inventory of their pain and suffering through a lifetime, they will carry on without ever truly knowing themself. I realized as a healer and curandero that I wasn't here to save or fix anyone else. I was here to heal myself and stand as an example of what transformation can look like, a wayshower, not a rescuer. Transformation is not futile sand running through your fingers. It is real. And when you really want it for yourself, you reach for it, grasp it, and hold on through the sometimes difficult ride.

I came to understand that I was worth the ride and if you don't want to ride with me, get off. The song "Ticket to Ride," by the Beatles came into my thoughts as I sat writing.

Over the years, I made efforts to achieve sobriety. It was a process of releasing and understanding solutions that didn't work. I tried to understand the why of my substance abuse. Someone gave me a book called "A New Pair of Glasses," by an Alcoholics Anonymous member named Chuck C. I began to scratch the surface of my why and believed I accomplished an understanding of myself and why I drank and drugged. But it wasn't until I set out on the path of the Red Road that I really began to understand from the place of my heart instead of my mind. My inner-standing and the concept of holding my vision or inner vision by seeing through "a new pair of glasses" changed my life forever.

"Blessed are the willing."
~ Walking Crow

Chapter 4: As Spirit Spoke

You might wonder how selfish or self-serving Walking Crow might be. But the truth is, if all of us had been taught to pay closer attention and had learned how to think and feel for ourselves, life might look very different. But that is not how life works. People can only pass on the information that was given to them. It's not that our parents and family were poor teachers. Through years of deep listening, I've come to understand that our minds, hearts, and thoughts are clouded by religious teachings and devotion a to church that has little to do with God as love, saving hearts, or truth - despite calling it salvation. I spoke out in their schools as I was fed the teachings of a god that doesn't even exist, not in my heart, my soul, or my belief.

After a lifetime of mind control, I was finally able to break free and say *YES* to a god voice, a god within me that speaks a totally different love language.

I came to believe that concepts and figures like God, Jesus, Mary, the Bible, and the rest of the cast in that book were often used as instruments of mass manipulation: tools for killing, plundering of cultures and peoples, stealing of properties and the vulnerable souls of humanity rather than as pathways to love. Like little obedient robots, many became prey to churches and institutions that claimed holiness but sexually molested and murdered children on every continent in the name of God.

I refer to my concept of a greater power than a church and call it Great Spirit. This is something I am comfortable with and find peace in. The church and government institutions spend a lot of time trying to make us be like them. We aren't. Innocent lives were taken, children sent to boarding schools run by religious institutions who made every effort to strip people of their culture, languages, and beliefs, killing and raping many in the process. They tried to break the spirit of those who only wanted to live as a sovereign nation on their own.

As I outgrew the old teachings and my beliefs, I found compassion for myself and for others. This wasn't true for everyone, because I didn't trust everyone. People came and went, lied, abused, and manipulated me over and over again, so why would I trust? It took many years of deep self-forgiveness to release what had kept me trapped, tethered, angry, sad, and full of self-hate.

You might ask, what does all of this have to do with *As Spirit Spoke* or with the voice of spirit? As I listened to spirit speaking to my heart, all those things I had been carrying were being filtered through slowly and painfully. Even when things felt dark or overwhelming, I started to believe more deeply in myself and in a Greater Spirit. That softened my heart and helped my inner-standing of both self-forgiveness, forgiveness of others and my feeling of honest love.

Learning to lean into deeper listening became primary. I began filtering out the static energies, voices, and monkey mind chatter. Removing the television from my living space gave the ears of my heart room to breathe. In that quiet, I could do the pushups necessary for close attention to develop and strengthen my intentions. This kind of listening was foreign to me, lol, of course it was - because I had been conditioned and colonized like everybody else around the world.

I began to understand the whisperings and physiology of trauma, hurt, and shame, and learned how they worked against me in my body, mind, and soul. My mind had been blocked for a lifetime as I didn't have the inner-standing of how my body's intake and living in my head or mind worked against a better way of being and doing. Every choice I once made grew out of the sickness of the voices I lived with, and my inner-standing became the key to my present and ongoing transformation. I have become void of all those excuses of bad behavior and now make decisions for my better good and only mine. Spirit whispered into my heart that *"You (others) are not my business until you say you are my business."*

My interference was not asked for or requested, so I understand I am my sole (soul) focus. The more spirit whispered to me, the more and deeper I became willing.

One day I heard *"Be in the doing of the being and the being of the doing."* I understood clearly what that meant and what it would mean going forward. Not just for me, but for those who were beginning to hear the messages I was sharing on social media and other places. I understood I had to stop trying, thinking, forcing my will, and wandering (wondering), and let go of futile prayers asking for the same things over and over again. I was asked to trust. My faith led me to eliminate a life of endless prayer, begging and groveling out of neediness and trying to keep up with the Joneses.

All this information and insight didn't appear overnight, it was a gradual process over years as I became and embraced my newness. I never knew when I was going to receive a clear message, but when I did, I inner-stood, embraced it, incorporated it, and began to teach and repeat the information I was given. I began to inner-stand that whether I prayed a prayer one thousand times or ten thousand times, it didn't mean spirit was going to answer when I wanted. After all, what did I believe in - or fail to believe in? I always say, *"God heard you the second time and said no, because **you** didn't believe **you** the first time."* I was being taught to be responsible with and for my faith and trust. I did and I do! Either I did or I didn't, either I do or I don't. My choice was clearly made, and my internal voice continues to grow stronger, deeper, and louder.

A lot of what I say comes in the form of profound questions that poke people right in the chest. Many still don't understand, but I don't feel the need to explain. Those that could, would, and they honestly wait for the next tidbit from spirit. I say to those listening, *"If I rub you the wrong way, maybe I'm rubbing you the right way."*

A woman I met in Sedona along the way asked, "What are you trying to say? I don't understand. Are you a provocateur?" I realized yes, I had become a provocateur in a most unconventional way by provoking people with spirit questions. I had never spoken like this before I stepped on to the Red Road, but I had never listened in this way either. The times in the ceremonial sweat lodge came to mind, where more was revealed every day. In the lodge, we were asked to say *palabra* (the word) before speaking and after saying that to sit in silence, because the next thing out of our mouth should be truth. This lesson I carried forward into my walk and life.

I have been writing down the quotes and statements I verbally share with others. I realize I have become a storyteller and am willing to share those, too. I never really considered myself a speaker or writer, but these are being channeled through me. As I accumulated more and more quotes, I began calling them "Crowisms." Why Crowisms? Because they were coming directly out of my heart and through my mouth - and I seemed to be the only one saying them. Calling them Crowisms was my way of being cheeky and lightly taking ownership of my words. Or maybe I should say responsibility for my words! I was posting them on social media with dramatic pictures of myself as a way to show people where these were coming from and who was speaking. I have compiled hundreds of these Crowisms and add hashtags to them so they can be found and referenced in the world of social media where I have developed quite a following - which didn't actually make me comfortable at first.

I've always said I don't own anything whether it is words, drums, rattles, healings, or stories. I've often referred to myself as simply a caretaker or a conduit of connection. I tell myself if my ego gets involved in what I am doing, I'm going to stop and walk away. I understand how far I have come and no longer want to entertain the ego of the old Anthony or Tony. I just wanted to be free of him.

But being free of the old self never really happens. I learned to live with everything about him and respond to what used to be triggers in a new way, in a way that isn't threatening, angry, or unloving. I became direct with my words, speech, and actions, like I said, sometimes rubbing others the wrong way. Understanding this, knowing that their triggers are not my triggers, I hope they find their own way, whether through me or somebody else.

I found myself living the metaphors of shedding the skin as snake medicine does and the trees letting go of leaves in autumn. Rebirthing is what the spirit world walked me through - at their pace not mine. I moved through the shedding just slow enough for the old skin to fall away and slow enough for the new way of being to stick and allow me to be open to the new skin. This was a cycle that continued and still continues.

I spoke more about my transformation as it became clear I am the embodiment of the elemental pathway of earth, water, fire, and air.

My way is not the way for everyone. There are many paths to follow and which of those would be for you, I believe will find you. My way was the right way for me. I have no fear of outcomes or when outcomes will appear. I was not in a *"Hurry for a flurry or a flurry for a hurry."* I understand there is no final destination - only the journey. And with that, I simply say, *"YES!"*

Saying *YES* opened up every state and dimension of my emotional world. This is something we almost never discuss, but it became essential for me to have the experiences, thoughts, and new way of life that only I could live. The path is personal; you have to discover your own. It doesn't come by collecting advice from friends, family, or strangers, or from posting questions to get one thousand stupid answers and two thousand worthless opinions.

The answers come from within, from the eternal, internal world of spirit if you are patient enough and brave enough to be vulnerable to the silence of listening deeply and following the sound of your own breath.

"Within each breath is a deeper silence."
~ Walking Crow

Chapter 5: The Silence of Listening

Creating a better world for myself meant I would have to create it on my own, seemingly alone but never truly alone. My embodiment is like the planets that make up our so-called solar system. Individual bodies or planets came together to become whole as one body with many parts and many meanings. I imagine that the sound of the universe mirrors the immense silence within our body and soul when we finally take the time to deeply listen and make the effort to experience it.

When I speak of hearing it isn't in an audible sense. It is in the feeling sense, and through the expression of new ideas and inner-standings that are eventually verbalized from me. It is a knowing sense as well. I remember when I came into my knowing, as absolute awareness. I knew things I had never spoken or known of before, not taught by books or teachers in this lifetime. I would wonder and wander for hours at a time asking myself, "How is it possible that I know what I know and have such a strong awareness?" I began to inner-stand that all of my meditations, hikes, drives, times on the beaches and in the mountains or wherever were serving me in ways that I had never comprehended.

Why would I? I was steeped in the noise and static energy of the material world and what I believed it offered, not knowing that it was keeping me stagnant, uprooted, and unrooted. I always felt that I was behind the eight ball and didn't have what other people had or couldn't accomplish what others could accomplish. I was complicit in my own failures and self-destruction. Feeling came back into my life as the truth of my truths were revealed when I stepped through the thin veil and said *YES* to the spirit world. Rev. Emma and I had talked about having a 'stepping through the veil' ceremony and giving me a spirit name.

But more than anything, my truths were internal conversations that came in the form of quiet; silence and listening beyond my normal hearing capacity. Hearing or feeling *YES* was magical. It didn't need, want, or ask for anybody else's permission, opinion, or advice. It was there, ready and unedited, ready for me to speak it. So I spoke it exactly as it came.

Learning to be in the stillness of my internal world was a new experience as well as an adventure. I gave up nothing to be in silence. As I believe happens to many who are willing to follow their own calling, those who I considered friends and family quietly fell away into their own way of being. I didn't chase them; I just let them be in their own understanding of what was or is their path.

After reading a book on mindfulness, I began to make more changes in my world. I had never heard of mindfulness, but going through the book, I didn't just read it, I internalized it and began living it in my daily life. I would rise from my sleep and greet the day, the sun and my face staring back at me in the mirror as I prepared to leave the house and be with the greater day. I would go for my morning walk, and what used to be a powerwalk for the purpose of exercise became a walking exercise in mindfulness. Before I began this practice, I simply walked, bypassing and overlooking my surroundings. I mean, I noticed things, but my focus was on my feet and the physical aspect of my body. I had no thoughts or cares about other things until the subtle shift came. Then I stopped to look around and take in my surroundings.

Greeting the sun began each morning along with thank you to my body for giving me a new day. This was a simple enough start to what became a daily practice of noticing, acknowledging, thanking, and listening in gratitude. What was I listening for? What was I going to hear? Why was this point in my life any different than any other part of my life? Well, as the old saying goes, *"Be careful what you ask for."* Noticing the animals, trees, sky, clouds, water, and simple things, I now greet them and listen to them as they answer back or call to me.

As I go through my day, I greet the trees that up to this point were just part of the backdrop, nothing to really care about. Little did I know they would respond to my greetings. In the beginning I didn't notice what was happening. But silent conversations started because of a simple change in my behavior, the simple act of acknowledgement. They began speaking volumes to me and every time I looked their way, I noticed something different. New growth, a place where a limb had been cut away, a broken branch, a bird's nest held safely in its branches.

The trees spoke to me because I noticed the beautiful bark wrapping its trunk, calling my heart, and I would speak to it and outwardly say thank you. Usually when I walked it was in the early hours and even as the sun rose, I was aware of the beams of light and sun piercing through quietly asking for my attention. I sometimes took pictures of what I saw, but all these years later I don't know where those pictures are. The visions and memories of those moments still live in and through me.

During those walks, I carried my medicine bag or mochila (as it is called in other parts of the world). When I went to the mountains, out in the countryside, or to the ocean I also carried my drum, always willing and ready to offer prayers in song with the sound of the heartbeat vibrating through my drum.

When I was at the Rose Bowl in Pasadena, I would walk and gather plant medicines such as sage, black sages, and other plants. I kept my drum close by in my vehicle and when I finished my walkabout and medicine gathering, I would take my medicine bag and drum to sit in the middle of a big field, offer tobacco to Mother Earth and all my relatives, smudge myself and surroundings, then smoke tobacco to open a further connection to the spirit world. I drummed and sang the songs the spirit world had gifted me. This was all part of my daily practice as well.

Years earlier, when I lived in Northeast Tennessee, autumn would catch me by surprise as I drove. I'd round a curve in the road and suddenly, there in front of me were groves of trees in full glorious splendor - reds, yellows, oranges, and maroons with multicolored leaves in spectacular, breathtaking beauty.

It was temporary, gone within weeks, leaving behind the quiet elegance of the bare trees left in nakedness. What remained felt ancient and wise, rooted deeply in the earth. Looking back at those experiences, I realized I bypassed them without fully understanding it. But apparently my heart and the eyes of to my heart didn't forget. The memories live on.

My awakening or as I really like to call it my "coming to" is the reason I can speak of those experiences as I do. Mindfulness has been ever present in the transformation of my life and allowed me to become "he who notices." The noticing wasn't in my head through my thinking. It was held squarely in my heart space, which over time allowed me to have a new vision that was directly attached to the power of subtle listening and mindfulness.

I was paying attention to the subtlety of the silent voice. This didn't only happen with trees, it happened with plants, flowers, animals, shadows, clouds, the sound and feel of the oceans and water ways of Mother Earth, the darkness, light, sound, and virtually everything I had taken for granted throughout my life.

Mind you, this did not happen overnight. It unfolded through the gradual awakening of my heart and soul. I expressed earlier in these writings how it first manifested within my body, how I paid attention to the voice of humans and their words, not only what they said, but to the truths or lies I heard them speak or even not speak.

I listened and began to hear far beyond what they were saying. I could read their body and sense where their truth lived or where deception hid. I could tell where and how they carried their pain. I came to inner-stand this gift as Owl medicine – the ability to look into the darkness of the soul and read what lies within.

Reading subtle energy and the silent messages it contains can be very powerful, and it became a very powerful part of me. This is no parlor trick; it is the emotional body and how it shows up. The more I cleared myself through deep inner listening, the more I could feel the power grow in my heart. Having the ability to forgive myself, love myself, and give myself selfcare was the mastery I was developing and how I was able to become a mirror for a heart of gold - my heart of gold.

Looking at others and having a knowing about them could be dangerous if not understood and treated with respect. This inner-standing helped me with discernment and respect for the experiences I was having. In the beginning, discernment was something that sometimes eluded me, but over time the guides and spirits gave me silent direction of discretion and inner-standing.

In the early days of my energetic transformation, I crossed invisible lines with people and said things even when they weren't asking. This is what immaturity does. But with resistance from those who told me to stop, that they weren't asking for a reading and the direction of spirit, this was soon understood. I matured and the excitement of my new-found gifts began to settle from my head to my heart and I was able to stop running when I couldn't even walk at that stage.

The power of the silent voice and letting go of my self-struggles became easier and easier over time as I listened to the wisdom of the trees, animals, and the whispers of nature. I was developing the inner-standing of the elemental world of earth, water, fire, and air.

I started paying close attention to the animal world and began learning what different animals mean in the spiritual world and what medicines they carry. Each animal is unique and has its own magic and meaning. I went for walks and when animals crossed my path or I crossed theirs, I stopped, paying attention with a deeper listening than what I wasn't audibly hearing or visually seeing. I tried to feel the energy of the birds, whether Woodpecker, Sparrow, Crow, Raven, or Goose. I understood that each one carried its own unique inner and outer language.

I purchased a book by Dr. Stephan Farmer about animal medicines and spirits. As part of my morning practice, I read about an animal every day, learning the basic principles of what a particular animal medicine meant to the author, who was a shamanic practitioner. When I got to the end of the book, I went back to the beginning and read it all over again. I did this for as long as I felt necessary and when the time came, I let go of that practice. I began to develop my own inner-standing of the silent language of communication with animals. The native and indigenous worlds also have their teachings on animal medicines, which I paid attention to as well. They made more sense to me over time.

What does the animal look like, sound like, feel like? How does it behave and does my feeling inside resonate with the behavior? I started paying attention to their practices as they coincided with the four seasons, the medicine wheel, and how they appeared to me in and out of ceremony. Many animals first appeared to me silently in the ceremonial lodge as I sat and prayed in the womb of Mother Earth.

Seeing the animal in darkness and then as the east door was opened and light from the sacred fire flooded in, I would see them in the steam rising from the hot stones. Those experiences offered the powerful medicine I needed to become transformed and whole as the pieces of my broken life came back together.

This didn't happen overnight. I buckled in and gave myself every opportunity to learn, adjusting my hearing for each of the different teachings in all situations, no matter where they came from. I always asked myself the question, "Am I listening from my head or my heart?" This allowed me to change focus from the external world to my internal world.

Listening internally meant I had to go beyond the beyond of the beyond, as deep as my soul was willing to go. I listened to the sound of my blood coursing through my veins, which of course I could do by listening to my pulse or heartbeats with a stethoscope, but I wanted to experience it through the darkness of inner-standing. Not just because it's science or in a book, but I wanted to become one with all things internal, and the strongest message I understood was simply "flow." Wow! It started to become that easy. I began to watch the veins on my arms, hands, legs, and feet and how the flow moved through my body. The body doesn't send out reports or verbal messages, it reacts to what is taken in and released, along with environmental conditions, foods, medicines, and toxins.

Subtle energy became the primary way I learned to inner-stand how the body communicates to the heart and mind. It reveals what is not always obvious, showing where emotional wounds originated and when they first took root. I came to recognize the time frame, or what I like to call ground zero, when trauma first entered the mind, body, or even the lineage.

> *"You can't help yourself until you help yourself."*
> ~ Walking Crow

Chapter 6: Passion for Myself

The more I listened, the more I learned that I was the center of what I was becoming and began to see and feel for myself in a way that had been foreign for a lifetime. I had always believed that a relationship or partnership was outside of me and I needed to find someone I could partner with for a lifetime. Then and only then would I be complete and whole.

The media paints a false picture of love, passion, and what romance with a partner is supposed to be. But this fairytale is not for the average person, it's for the fool who is ready to spend money they don't have in the belief that they will forever have someone as their own. This is not love, passion, care, or otherwise. There is no "supposed to be" in my world of love.

In the darkness of my remembering and growing out of my lifetime of dismantling (dismembering), I began to see, feel, and honor myself from a place I had never known. My life was always about someone else: "Do as I say," or "Do as I do." I always seemed to fall short of their demands - or should I say commands. I never thought about this, but now I wonder if they could hear themselves or even believed themselves.

Moving forward with the rescuing of the little boy I left behind many years ago, I began by recognizing I had been splintered for a lifetime. Many of us are splintered and remain this way through our entire life, never finding a way out of more painful cycles we chose along the way. We find ourselves choosing relationships that don't work, imbibing alcohol, drugs, and food, smoking, and being with people that are not good for us, all due to no or low self-esteem from life's traumas, hurts, wounds, and shame.

Selfcare was the key. I began to do things for myself. I began to choose me, offering myself better things, making better choices. I began to give myself better words, which became the motivation for my transformation toward self-healing and change. I kept my eye on the prize, looking ahead and inner-standing there was no going back once I began the process of healing the inner soul. My choice of words and choosing a new and better way of speaking became and still remains paramount. I would catch myself during conversations and make verbal shifts on a dime. There is a bible verse that says, "For as he thinketh in his heart, so is he." I heard or read this for years and never took it seriously until I paid attention and listened at a deeper level. I even began correcting others during conversations, healing sessions, and ceremonies.

I began to let go of the language and words shaped by my lineage, my family, relatives, friends, and teachers. I realized they no longer served me and probably never had. For most of my life, I had been stuck expressing myself through anger, fear, shame, and the traumas I had lived through. I started searching out helpful relationships that could recognize my old way of speaking had really been a cry for help, not something to be met with judgement or opinion. The world is quick to offer advice or opinions before actually listening and understanding. I know this behavior comes from their own unresolved trauma and pain; my guess is that this is a defensive mechanism to protect their wounds.

There had always been someone ready to tell me what I was or wasn't. In my new way of being, those voices were silenced through my continued change and growth. Mine, not theirs! I began saying things like, *"I am not your business, you are your business."* Mind your own business was something I said to my heart and focused on myself more and more. Neil Young's song "Heart of Gold" would come to mind and I would tell myself, *"Walking Crow, mine your own business and your own heart, do not mine the business of others."* Not minding the business of others helped me keep my eyes on my prize as I mined my heart of gold.

This way of speaking to myself and others warmed my heart as I developed my own philosophies and ways of speaking and living. *"Mine is not yours and yours is not mine,"* was an understanding I clung to. I began to inner-stand and speak out loud that the traumas, hurts, wounds, and shames that I lived and suffered through are not and have never been mine. I was not going to carry the burdens of my family's past on my shoulders or in a broken heart. Just because they said or did it doesn't make it true.

I started to water my garden of the little boy, the young teenager, the drunk lonely alcoholic who was never given a chance to grow on his own. I became passionate about what I was doing and started speaking out loud what the spirit world said to me. People would hear what I said and as I spoke more, I became fearless. I began to poke people in the chest with the words and quotes my guides spoke to me and found I didn't have to apologize for my words, as I found myself standing on a new foundation of truth. I became well rooted and well fruited as my vocabulary and heart expanded.

I began to feel whole within myself and my world. It was my world, no longer our world. My talk began to match my walk, and my walk reflected my talk. This is what true power looked and felt like to me.

No longer embarrassed to speak out, I spoke for me and no one else. When people engaged with me because of the things I was saying and believing, I embraced them with thanks and humility, as it was all still new to me. I was like a child in a garden, a toy store, or at Disneyland for the first time, with my eyes and ears open wide. I was in awwwwe…

I was never taught about passion, love, or how to care for the child within me, who by the way is still here and thriving. I use the word thriving because I don't want to just survive in this world. I believe there is still a certain amount of trauma involved with simply surviving. I spent a lifetime wanting to be picked up and held by somebody, anybody, but no one ever came. They were all the same, all just as broken as I was.

This recognition forced me to make changes in the choices I was to make going forward. The old guard had to go and there was no longer room for those who would not support my new way of being and becoming. If you were here to fix me or change me, you had to go and were only welcomed from a distance if at all. I don't care how much you said you loved me or how good the sex was or what you could or couldn't do for me, if you leaked toxicity, you were not coming with me. I am well and good, thank you! My life has no place for needy, and I just want to separate myself from that pack. I believe that "People who are needy never do anything about what they tell themselves they need." If that feels shitty, it should, but neediness taught me a lot about what I really wanted and continue to want for myself.

Remember, *"You can't give away what you haven't got."*

I always felt this to be profound. Opinion and advice have no place when you don't know what you speak about. These things come from ego and a lack of or no self-esteem. I suffered from this for a lifetime and didn't know how to come up for air. In sobriety, my sponsor would say to me, "When you share, it's like you are a sawed-off shotgun blast and everybody gets sprayed." That was hard to hear, but it was years before I could figure it out and find a different voice.

Walk, don't run is what I had to learn. Just because I had a thought didn't mean I had to say it. Not everything that came into my thoughts was for everyone else. Most of the time it was simply for me. I had to learn how to take my time and be gentle with myself. If this sounds like a lot of me talk, well it is, as I continue to believe and speak that "You can't give away what you haven't got." I had to acquire knowledge and the love to speak about it as well as live it. Talking about it is simply not enough. I sought out those with similar thoughts, ideas, and passion for change who were living out loud and coloring outside the lines in their own life.

Borders and parameters were always a problem for me. Not staying in my own lane and coloring within the lines was something I was criticized for, along with being told, "Walk, don't run." As a child going out on the school yard, I would immediately start running and would hear the voice of a teacher or nun shout out, "Walk, don't run." I'm sure I'm not the only one, but I believe little boys are built for running, jumping, climbing, and adventuring.

I once saw my aunt's sister at a family function. As she approached, she expressed her happiness to see me as she hadn't seen me since I was a little boy. During our conversation, she mentioned that she thought about me often, worried about the little boy who was made to sit still while the other children played at family parties and visits. She said she couldn't understand the reasoning behind that and confirmed that little boys should be allowed to play. That is one of my all-time favorite conversations. I understood that somebody was watching and cared about me, but kept silent because I was somebody else's child and she didn't want to interfere.

Trying to find my place in life meant trying to live somebody else's life. You hear it all the time - a parent bragging about how somebody else's kid is so great for this and that and their own is just a problem, blah, blah, blah, blah. Never a kind word for their own child. As an adult those memories rang too loud and clear.

In my new walk as an adult, I gave a talk one day and the spirits gave me a powerful teaching and example of what happens or mostly doesn't happen to us as children. There is a schoolyard game called tetherball. In tetherball, a circle is drawn on the blacktop which is a parameter or limitation that one has to stay in to play. A hole is dug in the exact center of the circle. A pole with a rope attached to a ball is placed in the center hole, the rope cut to the exact distance from the center to the outer edge of the circle.

The idea is simple - two children play against each other, each trying to wind the ball attached to the rope around the pole in order to beat the opponent. To me, this game is just ridiculous. There never appears to be a winner, and I believe it only teaches players to stay stuck within the parameters set by someone else. There is only one way to play and countless children have played - and continue to play - the same repetitive game. As long as they keep playing, they can't change the rules and remain trapped in a mindless cycle of limitations.

This is how your government, schools, churches, and the media want you to be, doing what they give you to do and limiting your mind and expression. But if you take a knife or scissor and cut that rope of limitation, you could play basketball, kickball, volleyball, four square, soccer, or anything else you want to play without somebody else's limitations and control. You expand yourself instantly without their permission. I freed myself from the bondage that was never mine and continue to work to keep myself free of the control of others.

Now I understand with all the roadblocks and limitations that this world presents over and over again, most people will line up as they are told and drink the Kool-Aid flavor of the day. So, stop and look around, listen, pay attention, and set yourself free from the self-loathing, self-hate, self-limiting propositions that come from the outside world and begin to speak, listen, and inner-stand the voice from within. The answers have always been within us; we've just been led astray by the control of others. Fuck their control!

My voice will not be popular in most circles, but I am not for most circles. I am an acquired taste, the taste I always was, that they tried to change and make into a worthless robot stuck in the slavery they offer, spiraling downward in alcoholism, drug addiction, food addiction, the endless pursuit of the perfect j-o-b (prison) and the rest, with no self-worth, self-esteem or the freedom to be as I was always meant to be.

What is it you want? Do you have dreams, do you have your own voice, or are you limited to the voice they gave you through their programming? Go ahead! Try to be free while you swallow the pills of television, government, religion, and the media. Vote how they tell you to vote, eat and take the poison pills they tell you to take. I gave myself to all of it for most of my life, but my consciousness will not allow me to do or be that any longer. I have transformed from a seemingly hopeless state of mind and body. I was never hopeless, I was only helpless, I asked for help and remained hopeful.

I will never let go of my belief that true living begins by going inward and learning to live from within. My heart is open, ready to love the little boy and the man as one whole being. As I began to love the little boy within and welcome him into the heart of the man I have become, my passion for the path ahead grew stronger and clearer.

I now understand what true love actually is. I speak of myself in the most loving nurturing way, as only I can and will. Because I am passionate about myself, I am able to be passionate and find similar passions in the outer world. Not everyone will see me as I see me and that's fine with me. My hope is they find their flavor in themselves and find a love within they had never received before. This is my wish and blessing to all people in all walks of life. Remember, you are the most important person in your life and please give love to you first before you try to give what you haven't got.

"When I hear and see the change in you,
I will know what you have come to believe.
But I also know
I don't have to believe what you believe for you to believe
and in that is magic."
~ Walking Crow

Passionate is something we are not taught to be about ourselves - or at least, I was never taught to be about myself. But as I grew older, my learning curve shifted and I found it perfectly okay to change my self-speak. When I began speaking openly in public, there was often a shock value that I paid little attention to, because I was speaking in ways most people do not speak. I gave myself permission to step out front and out loud. At first, this felt deeply uncomfortable, but over time my body, heart, and soul found their footing in my new world.

I ask you not to be embarrassed by your newfound voice and new way of being and living. You owe it to yourself to fully claim who you are - to present you to yourself on a silver platter with all the trimmings and to enjoy every bit of it.

"If you can't turn off the noise you can't turn on the soul."
~ Walking Crow

Celebrated Ancestral Buck

Chapter 7: Forgiving Me to Forgive Them

I always felt I'd go through my life angry about how things went for me and spent many years steeped in anger and self-hate, living in confusion with a broken spirit. I remember talking to myself, arguing with myself, not feeling or thinking anything about it and not knowing if anybody was paying attention. I remember being a funny looking kid with dark brown skin and crooked teeth, wearing short pants and black leather sole shoes with holes in the bottom. I have the memory of cutting cardboard and placing it inside my shoes so my socks wouldn't get dirty, wet, or develop holes in them. So many memories I had forgotten about until now. I spent hours by myself playing in boxes and building forts in the yard. I tinkered with tricycles, taking them apart and reconfiguring them into a new way of being. They ended up looking like what later came to be known as "Big Wheels."

The way I was in life wasn't something I thought about as a young person, except for the neighborhood pecking order and always being chosen last or not at all for the team sports we played in the neighborhood. Basketball, football, or baseball, I was small and didn't seem to have the talents for hitting, catching, throwing, tackling, or shooting a basketball. But I made every effort to do those things and when I wasn't chosen, I sat on the sidelines hoping for an opportunity to play. Every now and again somebody would get called home by a parent or go to use the bathroom, allowing me to step in as a substitute and giving me an opportunity to play.

As a kid, Saturdays were always for yard work, which meant I had to sweep as there were no such things as blowers at that time. My father would mow the lawn, and my older brother would edge. As soon as he was done edging, he would disappear into the house to watch TV and whatever cartoons were on at that time of the morning. I was always unhappy and resentful that my job took so long I couldn't enjoy TV like the others. I also had a sister Rita, but she never had to work in the yard. It was like that for girls, but she was much younger anyway. I can still feel that feeling and smell the scent of fresh cut grass. There was something special about that smell and it has stayed with me all my life. Despite my resentment of having to do a job that took longer, there was also a sense of pride. I remember looking at the yard and being proud that I had a hand in what I was looking at.

We had fig, plum, and peach fruit trees in our yard and a milpa where we grew corn. I remember that side of the house being much cooler than the other parts of the yard. The soil was dark brown and I remember it always being damp. We also grew beans in another part of the yard and along the back fence had Elephant Ear plants. They had huge leaves and were surrounded by beautiful green moss at the base.

I spent many hours as a boy in that yard and when I wasn't picking corn with my father, I was sitting in the plum tree eating sweet dark plums or scouring the ground for peaches that had fallen off the tree. I'd find peaches that were already covered in bees eating their delicious juice. I'd leave those ones alone to not get stung and move on to the next piece of fallen fruit, wash it off with water and bite into that massive peach. Wow! What a treat that was. Because of the water and the southern California sun, the plums and peaches were huge, juicy, and always seemed to be ripe and ready to eat. When I wasn't up in the plum tree during the long hot summers, you could find me laying in the cool damp moss under the leaves of the Elephant plants.

I often took time to walk in the milpa between the rows of corn, waiting for the corn to ripen so mom could cook it for one of her delicious meals or barbeques. It wasn't the normal yellow corn you would buy at the market. It was colorful blues, reds, purples, whites, and yellows all on one ear of corn. I remember it being really sweet and eating it with butter or margarine. I still feel the smile on my face and the feelings it gave me as a boy.

I don't remember ever sharing these moments with anybody else from the neighborhood or even with my brother and sister. There were only three of us at the time - the youngest brother and sister came along much later.

I still relish those moments in my walks and with my relationship to trees, plants, shrubs, and even animals. The medicines of the earth served me then. This haven or sanctuary in our yard was my place of peace away from the neighborhood and my resentment at not being chosen for teams and what seemed like those long hours of sweeping and yard work.

I have grown out of the resentments of my youth and continue to choose simpler things, including my relationship with nature which I allow to nurture me and my healing heart. As I made my way through midlife, I began to realize that Earth was my mother and the elements I am birthed from. To this day, I honor her and have learned to love the divine energies that I was angry with for so long. With earth, water, fire, and air I began to find my balance, my center, my alignment. I found and came into more of my adult self, moving away from the childishness I had lived in for so long. The broken child was becoming *whole* after a lifetime of *hole*, healing the unbearable emptiness that I drank, drugged, and resented over.

Mother Earth became my caretaker and I spent as much time as I could with her alone, not sharing my time with her with anyone. I began to understand that I was carrying an anger that was not, is not, and was never mine to bear. Being somebody who didn't know any better, I carried it for years.

The hurt was so unbearable I chose to carry it no more and began to shed the hurt through the tears and words of the little boy who is now a man. I don't apologize for my tears or my words. I began to take my place in the world and understand the life and death cycle of not only the elements of mother earth, but the emotional elements within my body and soul. It has been said I would die many deaths to become the curandero, shaman, healer, and enlightened soul that I am. And so I did - and continued to stay on my healing path toward transformation. Not just for myself, but for others as well. I have become an example of transformation and change by being vulnerable and standing in my power at the same time. The power isn't something society can give or take away from me. Only I can say yes or no to what the earth and the spirit world can offer me and so it is. I accepted and said *YES* to the man and boy I had never known, becoming whole and one in the process.

I found I had to forgive myself for all of it: the blame, my assumptions, anger, hurt, shame, trauma, rage, and all those things I carried in the deep well I call my soul. I just thought of the word well and how it can be used. I realize there was no wellness within the well of my soul for a lifetime. That is not a comfortable thing to admit for most people, but I am not most people, I am Walking Crow and have ascended from a life of hurt only to hurt no more.

I gave myself the freedom to use my words with the strength I have gained by forgiving myself for the suffering I caused by my own hand through lack of understanding. Letting others, like my mother and father, off the hook for my judgements of the things I didn't know how to understand. "To thine own self be true." I began to understand those words fully, allowing clarity for a future of happiness and freedom I didn't know I could have. It seems so simple, yet it took so long to understand and allow myself grace as a child of earth, God, the spirits, and the universal qi (energy).

I use the Ho'oponopono, a Hawaiian prayer of forgiveness "I'm so sorry, please forgive me, thank you, I love you." Not just to forgive others, but I used it to forgive the little boy and the man I had been. Allowing myself to understand the forgiveness I wanted for myself allowed me to forgive others without waiting for an apology or something else in return. Little by little, forgiving became easier and easier. I forgave myself for carrying the weight of the world - or at least my small part of the world - that was never mine to carry.

As I moved into the deeper darker layers of shadow work, I could see that my parents had their own past to overcome or suffer through. I began to understand their shortcomings and to recognize that they may not have had the capacity or ability to be present or to even know how to be parents. As I forgave myself, I softened and forgave them for even things I didn't understand. Forgiveness is forgiveness, you either do or don't. I just wanted freedom for my heart and soul. More than that, I wanted the same for my mom and dad and even though dad had crossed over some years back, I wanted forgiveness for him.

Over the years I had chosen relationships I should never have been in as I had no idea how to be in one. Honestly, once the sex settled down, I was only left with myself and my inability to be in relation in a good way. I'm sure there are plenty of people like that in the world and I wasn't alone in my inability. All you have to do is take a good look at the divorce rate in this so-called Christian nation. I forgave myself for my poor choices and began to discriminate regarding relationships. If I noticed red flags after meeting someone, I said no to what wasn't good for me.

Intimacy became more important to me, so I listened as they spoke and listened even deeper as I spoke. I began to ask and be clear about what I wanted, which I believe many have no idea how to do. Looking for Mrs. Right or Mrs. Right Now was no longer an option for me. My relationship with my heart and the reality of giving to myself became and remains paramount. Deeply listening to someone else's words, I would lean in to be clear of their meaning, truth, or uncertainty. My friendships became intimacy-based, with established trust. The people I chose and that chose me grew into loving relationships. Most of the people I am close to were - and still are - in committed relationships with others and I feel good about the trust their partners have in them and me. These are friendships I never knew how to have as there was always an underlying and unspoken want of a sexual relationship before.

These trust-based intimate relationships became a new way of being. I can talk about what I want in my life and my friends listen and mirror good information back to me. I monitor these friendships closely and continue to learn by watching how they move through their relationships. My hope is someday I'll have a similar experience, but until then I'll walk and not run and remain hopeful that I am making good decisions and walking a good path forward.

As I continued with in forgiveness, I became more and more comfortable in my own skin. I forgave myself for the self-abuse that came through intoxication, self-doubt, and low - sometimes nonexistent - self-esteem. My inability to trust others slowly began to transform into a different form of trust. I began to trust myself and in doing so, noticed that I had become trustworthy. My clients would tell me how safe they felt working with me, whether in ceremony, during healing sessions, or while birthing drums. I came to understand that if I wanted to be trusted, I first had to trust.

That trust was not just for me but extended to my faith in a Creator or higher power that I believed had abandoned me long ago. In truth, the only abandonment that took place was my abandonment of the little boy and man inside me and with that, my abandonment of faith.

In fact, the Creator, God, faith, universe, spirit had never abandoned me or left me alone. It was my broken heart that had abandoned my faith and didn't believe that God could or would help me in my sadness. As a child, we were taught the Catholic version of religion about suffering and going to hell, not about love or maybe redemption. The symbol of Christ hanging on a cross with a crown of thorns and nails driven through his hands after being beaten was my example of a god. I mean, priests and nuns wore those symbols as a part of their daily wardrobe.

In my grandmother's house there was always a red candle burning and when it was time to pray the rosary, which seemed to take hours to do, it was always dark and we were on our knees. It was those kinds of practices that fed us misinformation, letting us know on a constant basis that we were sinners and going to burn in a fiery hell. That kept me at bay and as a young person left a harsh impression on me. This made me not want to have a relationship with their god. There was no comfort available for me with teachings like that - or probably in any religion that was being offered up at the time.

Around the age of twenty or twenty-one Diane, a close friend of mine from high school, invited me to go to church with her and I said yes. I had never known anything other than Catholicism, with their teachings of suffering and being a sinner. I went. I don't remember the details, but I do remember returning on my own after being convinced by two people from the church that showed up at my house to accept Jesus as my lord and savior because I was a sinner.

There it was again: "I was a sinner." How is it possible that I am a sinner? Regardless, I went to that Baptist church and accepted Christ as my savior, was baptized and saved from a fiery furnace. Lol! Even today that language makes me laugh as being baptized didn't change my life. I was still drinking and drugging and fornicating, I mean, wouldn't you? I was just getting started.

I eventually fell away from that church and lived my life the way I wanted to live it. I was working in a studio teaching dance aerobics and fitness classes in my twenties. Diane would come to take a class from me now and again and one day, I think for my birthday, she brought me a bible. I accepted the gift so as to not hurt her feelings or seem ungrateful. But having my own bible didn't change anything, I was living the same life.

I was arrested for DUI (driving under the influence) after my father died and found my way to Alcoholics Anonymous through the courts as part of my sentence. Thanks to Judge Michael Knight! When I say thank you, I mean it sincerely as my time in Alcoholics Anonymous and my eventual sobriety gave me a new life, or at least the beginnings of a new life.

It was within this sober time of my life I met a woman named Jolinda and spent time dating her. She invited me to a church that she felt good about and talked about how open and loving it was. Those two words were the hook that caught my attention. She didn't insist that I go to church but simply extended the invitation and one day I was there. Jolinda eventually moved away to Monterey, California but we remained friends. Her leaving didn't mean I stopped going to church; I became a part of that church family and continued the growth I was experiencing.

Alcoholics Anonymous talked a lot about a higher power and that concept fell well on my heart. The version they were teaching me at church about a higher power gave me peace and a place to call my own. I attended that church for years and even became a sexton. I lived in the church parsonage and was the church caretaker, as the church was open twenty-four hours for those who needed a place to go when the bars closed at 2:00 a.m. This was started by the church's original founder, John Wells. I was married and lived with my wife on the property, becoming a vital part of the local community. I worked with community members, homeless people, alcoholics, and drug addicts, seemingly never-ending due to the twenty-four-hour open-door policy of the church.

My wife and I were the caretakers there for about eight years. Living like that can take a toll and I eventually tired of it. I also became disenfranchised with our marriage. We lived rent free in the parsonage as payment for the work we were doing. Our financial lives were not improving, and I wanted to leave because there was no advancement or opportunity to get ahead. I took a job in the technology field in TV and film, working as a salesman and procurement officer. I wanted out of my church position, but my wife argued, "Why do you want to leave, we don't have to pay rent?" She was not motivated to find work and I was done. I decided to leave the marriage and that position and move on. We divorced and I never looked back.

I found myself reading books by spiritual teachers, some of which I purchased while in that marriage. The more I read, the hungrier I got. I seem to have no limit when it came to my newfound spiritualism. Still attending Alcoholic Anonymous meetings and staying sober, I found the world of energy healing after a profound healing experience that I had.

I sought out a school for teaching me to bring those abilities to the surface. Enrolling in that school, I found myself living in the Highland Park neighborhood of northeast Los Angeles. It was a beautiful and sometimes dangerous older neighborhood of musicians, artists, writers, gang members, drug addicts, and the like. I worked to develop my healing skills and soon became an artist myself through my photography and creating Christmas ornaments with "Dia de los Muertos" (Day of the Dead) images. I made a lot of friends in the neighborhood and became a regular at the local coffee house Café de Leche, where I met people from all walks of life.

I joined a popular East Los Angeles band called the Mexico68 Afrobeat Orchestra. We played all around the Los Angeles area and in local clubs. While playing in the band, I became known for my healing abilities and clearing ceremonies and was sometimes introduced as the band shaman, which I thought was funny. I mean, who says that? But that's the way some of the band members saw and experienced me.

I also learned about the sweat lodge, which was a vehicle for deeper and more profound inner-standing of where the spirit world was taking me. As I moved through my newfound world of healing and spirituality, I began to let go of my earlier beliefs about God and became more and more empowered by the teachings and medicines of the natural world. I was beginning to understand my elemental journey as the make-up of who and what I am and have always been.

This was mind and soul blowing for a man who only knew one world, so to speak. I began to investigate my native roots and learned the origins of where my people came from, and in the process began to shed the teachings of the religions of the colonial world. I found my own voice within. I found I had something to say, and it was more than the everyday parroting of what the rest of the world was saying.

My inner voice became stronger. As I sat in daily silence, I was given more and more to say by the spirit world. These were quotes and sayings, what I now call "Crowisms." It was a way to speak to myself as I developed and stepped more squarely onto the Red Road and leaned into the teachings of my indigenous past, present, and future. The words were a way to poke others in the chest, allowing them to see, feel, think, and be in a different way. When I said these things, I never found myself apologizing for my words and I began to find favor and growth in the spiritual world, along with those who were listening.

I believe this was all happening as a result of setting myself free from the teachings and judgement of others, by forgiving myself for trying to live up to what they wanted and would force on me. My voice was becoming my own and the quieter I allowed myself to sit and be, the more spirit gave me powerful words to speak with messages for myself and others. I began to say things I never even had thoughts of before, things I had never been taught in this lifetime, and things I just knew.

I stepped into a world of *knowing* that was new and exciting to this man who had spent his life being quieted by parents, family, teachers, religion, media, and government. I forgave the little boy for not knowing and not being able to have his own voice as a child.

The more I found forgiveness for the boy and the man, the more I was able to forgive my parents and all those who seemed to trample on my fragile spirit and nature.

I found this kind of forgiveness didn't come from religion, churches, money, schools, or anything else. Forgiveness comes from inside, with the willingness to look at oneself, to forgive and care for oneself in truth through the lens of a healed heart, allowing love to be given and received openly and willingly. My belief is that forgiveness was the key and it had to start within as I embodied, loved, and nurtured the little boy and the man into wholeness.

"Look past the darkness into the light.
In the darkness you will find your way
and in the light you will find you."
~ Walking Crow

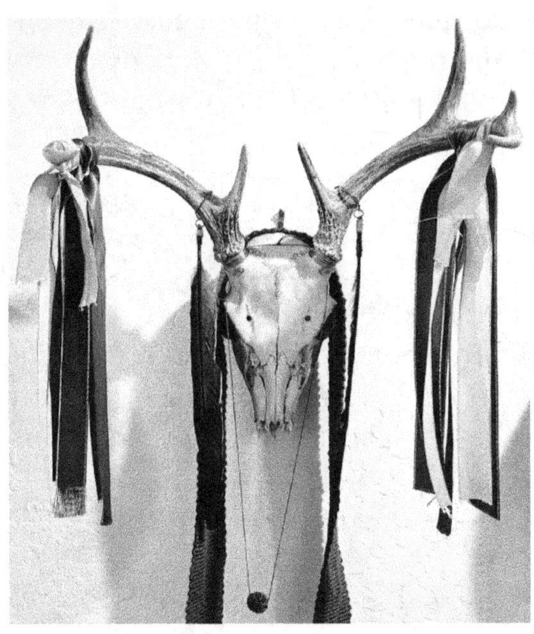

Shaman Healer Spirit Warrior

Chapter 8: Sitting and Walking with the Elders

For much of my life, the meaning of the word elder never resonated with me, nor had I ever even heard the term until I set out on the Red Road in my fifties. Even then, it took a few more years on my path before I paid enough attention to begin honoring what that word truly meant. Like most people, I assumed that elder simply meant older.

As I listened more deeply and felt into my own journey, it became clear that there was a vast difference. Clarity came when I started attending sweat lodge. Sitting in the sacred circle with the spirits and the elders who ran the lodge, I learned to listen in a deeper, more reverent way. They shared teachings I had never been aware of, but as I received their wisdom and took the messages in, I began to bloom like a flower opening to the light.

Whenever my elders spoke, I leaned into the message or voice. It wasn't just them I was listening to. I started paying attention to my surrounding world and Great Spirit began surrounding me with teachers who would not only speak but provide experiences that I never had before. I experienced actual listening, not just by me as their words washed over and through me, but I found them to be present in their listening as well. I didn't just hear, I felt heard.

Throughout my earlier life, I was always talking and not listening, talking in defiance and defense, never taking the time to hear fully or pay attention. My neediness and my mouth got me into constant trouble, never knowing when to be quiet. I always tried to talk myself out of trouble, while at the same time talking myself deeper into my own downward spiral. My self-importance was blazing hot and always ready for the battle without ever realizing I was losing the war.

The sweat lodge elders gave me a place of balance and seemed to slow down the pace of my brain or thoughts and emotions. They spoke slowly, precisely, and directly. I looked forward to our times together.

Within the classroom of the lodge, if I can call it that, they taught me to slow down by paying attention to what I was about to say. They did this by example. As we went around the sacred circle to give our name and where our people came from, we were asked to pause and say "word" or "palabra" which means the same thing in Spanish. After saying "word" or "palabra," we were asked to pause before we spoke.

The next thing that came out of our mouth as we readied to speak had to be truth or not spoken at all. I began to carry this practice into my daily life and as I moved forward on my path, my words and expressions changed. It became two-sided, not just me trying to be defiant or defensive, but to actually become interactive and present with others.

I learned that when I wanted to meet or speak with my elders, I had to ask permission and to offer tobacco as part of the potential conversation. The offering was part of the request for conversation. I started arriving for ceremonial sweat lodge earlier and earlier as there were tasks to do to prepare for ceremony. I chopped and stacked wood, brought out the blankets and canvases we were to use to cover the lodge, and took time to sit with the elders as the other men arrived.

Before I went for my first conversation with the elder Picos, I was asked to bring certain items and told not to arrive empty handed. I was asked to bring tobacco, water, a cash donation, and a covered dish of food to offer to spirit and the other men after we came out of the sweat lodge ceremony. I also contributed to the cleanup of the lodge area and the lodge itself, folding and storing the lodge blankets, and picking up any trash to not leave any trace behind except for the lodge itself.

From the beginning, the words spoken to me were invitations - how to arrive, how to attend ceremonial lodge, and what to bring. In time, these teachings became a part of my doing and my way of being present. The reminders were never spoken to me directly but were offered to the circle as a whole. As I listened and observed, my understanding and clarity grew clearer and stronger.

My elders held study sessions using the books of spiritual teachers. The protocol was the same, as we brought offerings and checked our speech and heart by saying "palabra" or "word" before speaking. We would also meet from time to time for breakfast or dinner at different spots around town, creating more of a bond with the men of the sacred circle. I learned to respect and love the elders of the lodge. Papa Luz, Hector (Macehualli), Picos, and Armando were the elders that laid down the path forward for me with regard to the Red Road and remembering my native and indigenous practices. I am forever grateful for those pillars who helped mold my being.

There were other elders from different areas in my life. Reverend Emma Molina-Ynequez is a wayshower, shaman, healer, and teacher. Master Sio is a Kahuna, master healer, and teacher from New Zealand. Jeannie Love is a mystic, guide, and healer. Those are just a few, there are many more who came along later in my walk, but these are the first steppingstones in the foundation of my evolution and the transformation of my soul and spirit. With these teachers, my elders, and spirit I began to open to new worlds and ways of being.

Many walks and talks, breakfasts, lunches, and dinner gatherings were a part of my evolution. More and more of my time was spent with the elders I learned to listen to, appreciate, respect, honor, and love.

It didn't end with these elders as I began to understand the relationship or lack of relationship with my mother and father. I could see and understand how I separated myself from my mom as a result of the things dad said to me as a child and how I separated myself from my dad because of his alcoholism. It wasn't until many years later, after my dad died, that I came to know and understand his pain which was the reason for his words and alcoholism. I was able to come to an understanding and compassion for the faults and inequities of others, especially my mother and father who I now look at as my most divine elders. I see them and hear them with eyes and ears of forgiveness and compassion and have learned to offer the same to myself and others.

As I walked the Red Road, I began to listen to those on social media who had teachings I wasn't aware of. I was asked by a sister, Anna Chio, Gentle Thunder, whether I had drums available for purchase. She spoke of an event that was going to take place in Blythe, California. I had never been to or even heard of Blythe, but she explained that the "Star Knowledge Peace Conference" was going to be held there and she wanted to purchase a drum to take with her. She also said that I had to be there. This wasn't just a request; it was a direct statement or demand. I said I would be there and spoke about it to my social media audience. They supported me all the way. This was my first journey of saying *YES* to my travels across the country with my drums and my newly remembered medicine journey. I don't really remember why I said yes as there was some fear surrounding her talking to me this way. I laugh now, but I was truly scared and nervous. I had never been to an event like this before.

I arrived there prepared for I don't know what, other than vending my drums. I was greeted by elder Terri Rivera as I knocked on her motel room door. I found her laying on her bed playfully singing. I introduced myself and offered a bundle of California White Mountain Sage that I purposely brought to offer as gifts. As Terri and I stepped out to the parking lot to get better acquainted, another elder dressed in native attire walked up and introduced himself and his sister. This was my first encounter with Uqualla.

Jeva Uqualla was with his sister who was simply introduced as "Sister." These were elders from the Havasupai nation of the Grand Canyon. It was an honor as I had never met native peoples outside of Los Angeles, who usually called themselves Mexican as I did. Anna eventually arrived and offered me the back of her truck to sleep in as the motel was fully booked with other participants for the event. She said I could use their bathroom for showering and such which was a generous offer. I felt I was already in that sort of giving spirit simply by saying *YES* and thank you and offering the sacred medicine of sage I was giving as I met others for the first time.

I met elders, brothers, and sisters from all over Turtle Island from different indigenous nations. I felt a little out of place as I had just started my journey to remembering my people and my own medicines. I guess it hadn't yet sunk in that I was native or indigenous. The first day of the festival, I made a point to visit every vendor to introduce myself, offering the California White Mountain Sage to all I met. My discomfort was overwhelming and I didn't attend many of the events at the weekend gathering led by Chief Golden Light Eagle. I felt like such a fish out of water that I failed to introduce myself to the Chief.

I met many beautiful souls over that weekend and exchanged contact information with vendors, healers, and teachers alike. The event left an impression on me, but I didn't know what to do with it. I should say that Anna Gentle Thunder did purchase a drum and all the drums I brought with me were sold on the first day.

It wasn't until four years later that I attended another event that I traveled to. This was another Star Knowledge Peace Conference, held in Peebles, Ohio at the Serpent Mound for the Spring Equinox. I had never traveled by car this far before, but it was the first of many journeys across the country that led to my life exploding with new relationships and friendships, meeting elders, Chiefs, Grandmothers, Grandfathers, Uncles, Aunties, and others. I was greeted with open arms, warm embraces, handshakes, and smiles as if they had just seen me at dinner last week. It engendered different feelings than I had from my first experience.

An encounter that I will never forget was when I stood at the entrance way of the event hall mingling with others when Mathew Campbell (Blue Hail Man) walked in. He is a gentleman I hadn't met at the first conference, but when I saw him there, he was leading the drumming and singing on the powwow drum as we sang and danced around the men. This singing and drumming was a wider introduction to becoming even more open to my walk. When Mathew saw me in Ohio, he approached me and greeted me with a huge hug, lifting me up off my feet in the most beautiful way. I had never been greeted like that by another man and felt honored and welcomed into the fold. Not that I wasn't a part of the fold, it just felt so warm and welcoming to be home. A little bit later as I stood at that same spot, Matthew took the Eagle Wing fan he was carrying and washed over me with that glorious medicine and cleared me by blessing and brushing me with those sacred feathers. This brother/elder and his acts I will never forget.

I became a part of the whole simply by showing up and attending the first event. I met and became friends with many of the elders: Matthew, Grandmother Beatrice Menase Kwe Jackson, Grandmother Barbara Vitale, Tata Arthur Cushman, Terri Rivera, Thomas Johnson and many, many others. I listened to their teachings as much as I could, which wasn't always easy as my tent for vending was outside the building and I had to tend to it. I was also given the opportunity to speak at this event which opened my heart to a new level. Feelings of acceptance and happiness washed over me in a way I had never experienced before.

Traveling across the country allowed me the opportunity to meet and stay with people I encountered over the years on social media as I was invited to stay as an overnight guest with their families. I was honored by both the invitations and the experiences. This allowed me to meet and develop relationships with children, husbands, wives, and neighbors. Everywhere I went I was welcomed. I was not only meeting elders and building community, I was also becoming part of a spiritual family that stretched across Turtle Island. Through my travels, I was also learning how to step into my own role as an elder to others, cultivating trust within many different communities along the way.

Whenever I pass through Kansas City, I am invited and welcomed to stop by Alejandra (Alex) McAnderson-Villa Lobos and Maria Al-Rubaie, both of whom I consider daughters. We first met in Sedona when they reached out to receive drum medicine. That connection eventually led to an invitation to hold ceremony for them at a spiritual retreat they were hosting. It was another invitation I could not and would not pass up.

These two women honored me deeply. Alex began calling me *Uncle* and Maria called me *Papa Crow*. Those names carried great meaning for me. I was invited into their homes and welcomed to stay with them alongside their husbands and children. I developed deep relationships with the whole family and was welcomed as a family member. Alex and I offer healing circles when I pass through town, and I sell my drums and rattles. More importantly, I was developing community and again…family.

Along the way I accepted invitations to different spiritual events like the Gathering of the Elders hosted by Grandmother Susan Stanton. As a result of me saying *YES* to attend her event, she became a close and trusted friend, ally, and elder. She introduced me to more elders and relations from all over Turtle Island and around the world. This was the largest event I had attended to date and one of the most important because of the relationships I developed through it. Such a depth of community from all four directions of the globe.

Sedona had been yielding new relationships as well. At first, I spread myself thin and tried to reach out to as many people as I could, but as in life this doesn't always mean those we meet will become friends, allies, or elders. I reeled my tentacles in as some who called themselves friends fell away or moved. Sedona, it seems, is a very transient place and not all who are called or say they are called will stay for many reasons.

I began spending more time isolating, not necessarily to stay away from people but more as a preparation or a filter. I was ready for those I would eventually encounter who carry their own brand of wisdom and medicine to share with me and others. The pool of those I could meet was smaller in Sedona, but the depth of the person and soul was more revealing, and I became a friend to those who would accept me for simply being me.

Saying that, there are many friends I miss. They have not died or passed on, but simply made the decision to pass on me, which has nothing to do with me as we are all different and come into each other's lives for whatever amount of time or reason. I don't believe anything is forever.

One of the things I learned along the way was to honor an elder at whatever place they are. If you are a grandmother, grandfather, chief, native elder, auntie, uncle, sister, brother, niece, nephew, or friend there is a place of honor and love within my heart. But in case I fall short, hello human, please forgive me as I continue to evolve.

My sacred circle in Sedona is small and those who are within the circle know how much I love them. Whether it is in conversations, meetings, over coffee, a meal, a donut, or through a healing, I live in gratitude for those who I see and those who see me. There are those who express love for me and those that don't - as we don't know how to do all things all the time. I hold no expectations. I have surrendered to myself, the world, and spirit and have become open and willing to meet all things as they are.

This is what I learned from my relationships and through the teachings of the elders on my path along the way. For this, I am eternally grateful.

"Undoing my life is rebirthing my soul."
~ Walking Crow

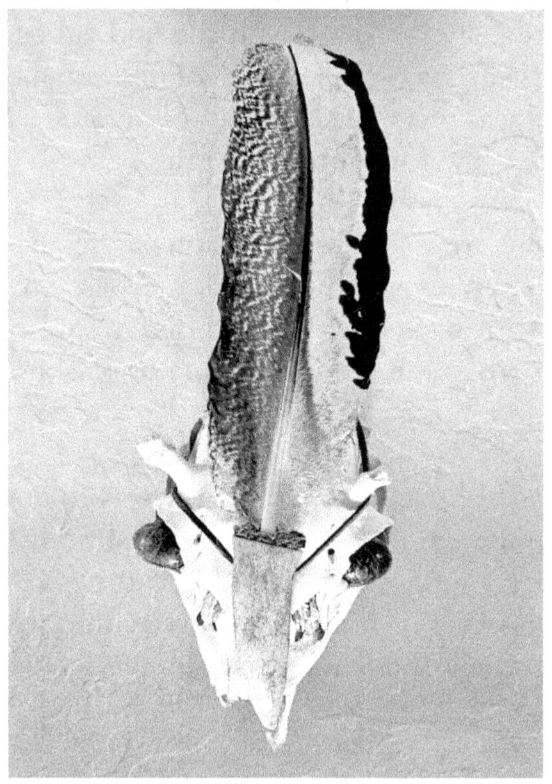

Canyon Spirit Guide

Chapter 9: The Trust Within

There was a period as I was getting sober that when I got home from an Alcoholic Anonymous meeting, the time alone was so loud and overwhelming that I would turn on all the lights, the television, and the radio and get on the phone. I was always wanting or having to be stimulated by something - especially something outside myself. I didn't know what stillness or peace was and I definitely didn't know how to source it or seek it out. I mean, how would I? It felt like the monkey mind or static was always running in my head. The same energy that got me labeled as a hyperactive child and got me into so much trouble growing up was still with me without any way or means to control it. Even as I was sitting in morning AA meetings, I found myself talking and causing a disturbance while others were sharing. This kind of behavior got me dirty looks and remarks. I still didn't know how to stop.

I had been speaking and acting out all my life with no awareness of how I was disturbing others, even when I was called out, punished, and sent to the principal's office in grade school. It only got worse in high school as there were more people and minds to create disturbance with. I found others who rode on the edge of trouble, who seemed calm on the outside but were hell raisers on the inside. I was that. I was a hell raiser and had found my people.

As a teenager I always had a parttime job, so I always had money for expendables like food, alcohol, pot, and gas. The guys I usually hung out with were from school or from when I worked at McDonalds. On the job we were fun and liked to kid around, still doing our jobs well. But there was always an undercurrent, a feeling that something was brewing. We would get together at night for tackle football games and play for beer. The problem was, we were dangerous. Not only to ourselves, but to each other. We would tackle or hit each other so hard we limped or were in physical pain for years. All this roughness and physical pain never got in the way of our friendships or jobs.

There were nights we would get together and meet at the high school, where it was common ground and there was nobody around but us. We would walk the campus just hanging out. One night a group of about twenty guys gathered at the school, climbed the fence, and decided to run around and raise some hell. There was a driver training simulator trailer parked on campus and we got the wise idea to push on it from one side until it tipped over. And it did. We whooped and screamed with excitement after tipping it over, then piled up in each other's cars and left. Never heard anything about it after that night.

This isn't something I'm proud of, but it is part of a larger story about what it means to be unable to find stillness within. In class, I always found a comrade or pal to disturb a classroom with. Other kids laughed, but it was probably an uncomfortable laugh for the fool causing the problem. I was always quick witted and funny, or so I thought. So much so that I was voted "class clown" and "most likely to drive a teacher insane" along with my friend Kathy. Obviously nothing to be proud of, but it was the short end of a stick of recognition and I accepted it. Looking back, it was the obvious acceptance of the lonely child. I mean, who could or would want to be proud of that? But I accepted it proudly and sadly moved on in my life. And though I said sadly, I never wore the face of sadness on the outside.

I left high school, but not how most people leave high school. I had taken an assistant manager's position at the local tire store and had to be available to work days, so I just walked away from school. I didn't have any reason to stay as I felt out of place in that environment anyway. In fact, I was never comfortable in school, but my parents and teachers didn't seem to care. It felt like they only cared when they received a phone call or they were inconvenienced by having to show up regarding the troubled child. I say this now, but that's what it felt like at the time.

I was flunked in the second grade because of my troubles and my tribe moved on without me. I wasn't alone in this as others in the class were left behind as well. I'm not sure how they felt, but there was a lot of uncertainty and loneliness around it for me - especially when my brother and the older kids at school made fun of me. The faces of the other kids in my tribe that moved on became invisible to me.

A similar event occurred when I was in high school. After settling into my new tribe, we moved together through grade school, first through eighth grade. From there, we moved on to a four-year high school, ninth through twelfth grade. However, my parents came to me during the summer after my second year and said I wouldn't be going to that school anymore because they couldn't afford the tuition. So I was moved away, separated from my tribe again, thrown into public school and the unknown. I honestly believe that as much as I tried or didn't try in my new surroundings, the end wasn't far off. When I finally walked away and dropped out, I didn't consult with anybody or ask for anyone's opinion. I just quietly left, never to return. Nobody came looking for me and my parents never questioned it. And so it was.

My time was spent working at the tire store as the assistant manager. Frank was the manager and a nice enough fellow. He seemed fairly young and I was confused by his character as he was a guy who came from means. His family had money and lived in Santa Barbara. I don't remember how long I worked there, but I remember receiving my paychecks and being able to buy nice clothes and fine colognes. I was always well dressed - had to be for my position. Over the years I moved from job to job, never staying in any one place too long. I would move on for better pay, but at some point that all stopped. It was the eighties and even though I drank, I heard about cocaine and how you could make money selling it. So I sought out those that would supply it and off I went for the next five or six years making money at first. Then came the downward spiral.

I remember working as a stock clerk at a supermarket and going to work intoxicated from alcohol and cocaine. I don't even know if anybody noticed as I worked from 11:00 p.m. until 6:00 a.m. I do remember being glad when morning came and my shift ended. I was eventually living like a drug addict with my brother and life was a party until it wasn't anymore. My brother lost his house and car and found himself in rehab. Me, well I just walked away from the drug life and moved on, which seemed to be my way of doing things. Just walk away.

This didn't mean I stopped drinking, it only meant that I ended my drug life which I attribute to my upbringing, loneliness, low self-esteem, and a lack of love for myself and being cared for. When I was arrested and sentenced to twenty-six meetings of Alcoholics Anonymous, I had no idea I would get sober and stay sober. I mean, why would I do that?

But over time I did stay sober. I didn't realize it, but something was happening deep inside me that wouldn't show itself for years to come. It changed the course of my life in a profound way forever, whatever forever means.

Staying sober through multiple decisions to get married and moving from job to job, I eventually came to a place in my life and sobriety where I tuned into my listening and heard a voice speak to me that changed my life. I had been taking classes to learn how to tap into my healing abilities and as I sat in a meeting of Alcoholics Anonymous for the last time, I heard a voice say, *"Listen to the still small voice, not to the voices."* I looked around to see who was speaking to me and there was nobody sitting near me. The voice repeated itself and I realized it was coming from within me. *"Listen to the still small voice, not to the voices,"* it repeated. I got up and left Alcoholics Anonymous and never went or looked back.

This was the beginning of doing things differently, listening and making decisions and trusting me, myself, and I for the first time ever. I first got sober on January 26, 1992, and for twenty years sat in meetings evolving as a human and sober man but not really going anywhere. I realized I had been raising my hand and proclaiming my alcoholism and calling it in day after day after day claiming it. I wasn't allowing myself to be free from the torment and bondage of the obsession of the mind and the allergy of the body, two key components of alcoholism. I no longer had either and no longer suffered from a spiritual malady. I began to change my words and spoke to myself, of myself, and for myself in a healthier way, giving myself new words and substitutions for the old language and words.

I listened harder and deeper. Not to the outside world, but to a world I had ignored for a lifetime. My inner self and voice. The child I had left behind was calling out to me to listen and pick him up and I began to be the caretaker of my heart and soul at my own behest. Rescuing that child and merging him with the man was paramount. There he was, the little boy standing in front of me looking so small with his arms raised in the air, fingers and hands opening and closing asking to be picked up. I felt into myself and without hesitation I crouched down, put my arms around him, picked him up and held the boy tight asking for forgiveness.

With tears streaming down my face, I swore never to let him go ever again. I whispered how much I loved and missed him as he hugged my neck, tucking his head under my chin as his little body trembled from grief, tears, and happiness. After a lifetime of disconnection, loneliness, and unhappiness, here he and I stood becoming whole and one for the first time through the tears of forgiveness.

During this time the spirits woke up inside me and what felt like a landslide of information, feelings, and thoughts came rushing forward. I spoke the words spoken to and through me. I became a vessel and a conduit of the voice of transformation with the willingness to give myself whatever necessary to grow, change, and become.

Transformation had begun to take shape over the years as I began to say *YES* after the life of *no*. What I would be shaped into, I had no idea. But the feelings were like a warm bath on a cold night or tasting something delicious for the first time. I was held in such comfort and safety, I found myself wanting more and more. I readjusted my focus squarely on the road ahead and the voices of spirit inside.

If you've never taken the time to listen deeply, you may be surprised by the messages and the truths that come through, truths that can guide you toward freedom, if you are willing to listen and follow simple directions. I began writing down the messages I was receiving. Sometimes they came in songs spoken in strange and what seemed like ancient languages, mantras, short quotes, or downloads during ceremonies and healings. One of the mantras that was given to me was to help me get centered, grounded, and aligned. It is called "I am where love lives."

I am Where Love Lives

I am where love lives and I am what hope looks like
I am where love lives and I am what hope looks like
I am where love lives and I am what hope looks like

You are where love lives and you are what hope looks like
You are where love lives and you are what hope looks like
You are where love lives and you are what hope looks like

We are where love lives and we are what hope looks like
We are where love lives and we are what hope looks like
We are where love lives and we are what hope looks like

There is no you without me and no us without we!

~ Walking Crow

This is just one example of how listening and receiving took place as the spirits spoke to me. The more I listened, the more they spoke, the more I wrote down and spoke and sang, the more they gave. Through the social media of the day you can find hundreds of sayings and quotes that I channeled from spirit - songs, poems, verses, sayings, and teachings. Those who were listening started referring to me as a wordsmith, which I found funny and flattering at the same time. Funny because I was never considered smart or intelligent and I would never dare to speak of myself or accept myself in such a way because of ego. But the other shoe dropped, and I accepted my role as a wordsmith of sorts and began to call the things I say *Crowisms*. These are things that nobody else said and are solely attributed to my life, mind, heart, and voice - really just me and my willingness to change and share the concepts of my own inner-standing.

Over and over again the spirit world spoke as I became willing to inner-stand the importance of the simple acts of listening and being still. You cannot live and move in the static energies of the world and tell me how much you know. I will look at you directly and listen to your words and I will know - as I knew and understood these things about myself.

Unplugging from the static world did more for me than any church, teacher, guru, master, or everyday know-it-all. I began to see those who never stop talking for exactly who and what they are. The broken child within that had to be noticed, in the middle of the room, who bought their own press more than anybody else. I believed in myself and my words until I didn't believe me anymore. The veil had gotten thinner and I was exposed.

I believe the quieter I got, the more I was given and the more I learned. I did not always share the insights given to me as most of the time they were only for me and my own growth or betterment. Seeing yourself and calling yourself out is uncomfortable because others might notice and call you out as well. Oh my gosh, they know! It was never a concern of mine as I was my harshest critic and worst enemy.

Years ago, a female friend of mine asked, "Why don't you stand up straight?" I was 30 years old at the time and had no answer. I made an effort to stand up straighter and walk tall but couldn't maintain that posture due to the low self-esteem I carried for years. It wasn't until much later that I found myself feeling happy and holding myself straighter upright. Sobriety had helped me through the years, but it wasn't until I set myself free and stopped holding myself hostage through blame and self-hate. These are hard things to admit and see within myself, but that's the plain truth.

I wasn't hard on myself once I understood and began to care for myself with self-love. I had no idea whether others could see the difference with the changes of my life, but I knew, I could feel the changes. I prayed for the willingness to carry on, even when I was tiring of myself. I mean how can a person be so consumed with themself? Well, I was. I don't believe it was in a narcissistic way, although I was truly consumed. I understood that I wanted and needed others to allow my new role and way in life to unravel and take form.

I couldn't shake the wanting to know or care about what others thought of me. The desperate and lonely child was still just beneath the surface. How could I stop wondering or caring about what others thought? It was over time that my obsession with what others thought of me slowly drifted away. Treating others like I wanted or thought I should be treated was one of the answers. I became a kinder, gentler soul just by simply making the effort. Really? It was that easy?

Yes, it was and is that easy!

Words became a vehicle of change whether I said them out loud or silently to myself. Slowly over time, transformation took place due to my complete willingness to give myself something different, to allow myself to develop a healthier ego and love for myself.

It is said, *"You can't give away what you haven't got."* So I began by giving to myself all I could so that I could become not so much a gift to others, but a gift to myself after a lifetime of believing I had nothing to offer. I turned to social media and began sharing my words and experiences almost daily. Until then, I never realized how much I had to say or that I even had the ability to say it.

I was given the opportunity to host my own radio show online and I said *YES*. I didn't have a huge listening audience, but the time on air allowed me to come into more awareness of my intuitive and psychic nature of knowing.

I let go of fear, nervousness, and stage fright. Almost everything I did was in front of others except for my personal practices. You've seen renderings or had experiences of cats when they are in the posture of fear with their backs arched and hair standing on end. That was me all the time. It was simply a matter of time before you noticed I was scared and in fear. The more I spoke in front of people, though, the layers of internal and external fear melted away.

The radio show and videos I was producing helped me in the biggest way. I couldn't see or hear the audience unless I allowed call ins. It was me and the microphone and the lens of the camera and I knew they were not judging what I was sharing from a deep place. Bravery and vulnerability became my bedfellows as I moved along.

This arena taught me how distance between us could not cause me harm. When I was on stage with the band in front of hundreds and sometimes thousands of people, I made the decision to play my instrument, sing, dance, and just have fun. This was the experience of freedom, the feeling of not worrying about thoughts, doubts, or judgement from others. I would float behind the microphone in my world of bliss.

In the early days, when I was singing kirtan and listening to teachings from the Gita on Wednesday nights, I would hear Swami talk about God from his point of view. One night I heard him say *"God is simply bliss and nothing more."* I heard those words and it was like my heart exploded. I was set free from a lifetime of pressure and pain of trying to live up to or measure up to something I had failed miserably at. Bliss! God! This simple connection was all I needed for happiness and self-awareness. I had become, I had accepted, and I was aware. Nothing could take this feeling of happiness from me.

I attended those sessions at different temples and in homes with people who looked different than me. I listened to the teachings even though I couldn't fully understand them and I would sing the songs of praise not knowing the words or language. The language of the heart is what I began to understand and latch on to. I was fed and nourished with food from a foreign land in the physical and the spiritual and I feasted to my fill.

It was okay that I didn't understand or identify fully. I was the student, I had appeared, and I was ready to sit at the table in bliss. This is the same feeling I get standing behind the microphone on stage or in my studio speaking to what I think is nobody but realizing somebody is always listening, even if it's just me.

"I am the I am that I say I am,
you don't have a horse in this race"
~ Walking Crow

Chapter 10: The Long Walks

I found that mindfulness and calm filled me more as I chose to walk my path, not just physically, but emotionally, spiritually, and I will say eternally. The bonding that took place as I walked through daily life forged a new way of being. My life was an array of so many pieces that I had no idea which way was up, down, North, East, inside, or out. But the pieces knew, they knew how they were to come together for my better good and soul. The most important component was the space between the pieces that drew them together like magnets. The observer had become transfixed and willing to notice the transformation, transition, transcendence, and transmutation of the boy, man, soul. I realized I was my own witness!

This revelation gave me an insight to the healing of the heart, mind, and body revealing answers that were hidden from me for years. As I went on my walks in the early mornings I spent time with this focus. It was mindfulness that slowed me down and gave me the 'walk don't run attitude.' Whether I said it quietly or out loud, my inner voice was asking me to just slow down.

My long walks with Emma served me for the same reason. Those walks weren't just for just exercising our bodies, but our hearts and souls; it was the space between us that brought us together on the pathway to healing. Asking questions and listening for the answers from Emma's heart, I hung on to her every word and the thoughts she expressed, as if it was a magic elixir that would cure the sickness within. Listening to her on those long walks gave me permission to say *YES* to my own voice after a lifetime of nos.

Never being able to fully express myself as a child or young adult filled me with a rage I could never clear. Where would that ability come from or even the words? The ability had been taken away from me - or so I believed. My mother called that rage in me ravia. I hated hearing that, but all I would do was get angrier. It was repeated over and over again that I had "el diablo metido" (the devil in me). What a thing to say about your own child! And then to do absolutely nothing about it but condemn with those kinds of words. My long walks with Emma began to change all that, with a present-day opportunity to make and experience life-changing decisions and behavior through the love and gentleness of another that didn't judge me.

Walking with friend and teacher Master Sio held the same experience, but our interactions always began with sharing a meal. When we were finished eating, we would go for short walks through the neighborhoods adjacent to the location of the restaurant we chose. Sometimes it was just pizza at Costco in the food court, but a walk and continued talks were always part of the agenda. Emma and Sio both had their own take on our discussions, and I always came away with new and valuable insights which allowed me to grow from the stagnant position of the past.

I also walked with friends around the canyons in the hills and mountains in my surrounding area. Most days I walked alone, but other days with a friend. The walks and hikes were adventurous as many of those trails I hadn't walked before and most of the experiences were new. When joined by friends, there were many conversations about daily life and healing as some of them went to the same healing arts school as I did and we found commonality in our stories of pain and healing. In some of the canyons there were no trails or we would go off trail into the unknown and blaze a trail of our own, which I believe mirrored our life's paths.

Trusting we were safe without having to know our way forward, we began to trust ourselves and keep going until we found the smallest hint of a trail to make our way back. Those walks and conversations allowed me to tap into trust. Not just of the trail and what I could or couldn't see, but trust in the human or spirit walking with me. I always felt safe and guided to trust my intuition and the nature within. As I began to trust the nature within, I also began to nurture the nature and believe I was trustworthy to myself and others. Over time the voices that rang in my head about what a terrible child I was or how I had the devil in me began to fade as I heard new voices and loving words more and more.

As I walked on the earth and my limbs connected with those energies, I became grounded in my body just by doing and being. I didn't have to make up stories about what I had to do to be grounded. I was just grounded, the more I allowed myself to openly receive Mother Earth's energy through the amazing gift of the body and legs I was given. I wasn't in the habit of arguing with my inner self about whether I was or wasn't grounded. I just was and didn't have to prove it to myself or others. Saying *YES* to myself after a lifetime of no removed the fear of the unknown.

This didn't mean I wasn't going to make mistakes or make wrong choices. It became a roadmap of how not to get in over my head while making decisions and developing new ways of seeing situations for my better wellbeing and developmental growth. I made decisions about my life and when things didn't go the way I wanted or expected, I didn't beat myself up or call myself stupid. I simply said to myself, "Hi human," and giggled. This was something my AA sponsor would say in my early sobriety when I was bitching about my life. He would simply say, "Hi human," and laugh at me, which in turn made me laugh at myself. I let go of taking myself so seriously, which in AA we called rule 62.

Emma was a major sounding board for me as she had seen me through a relationship and my last marriage. In fact, as a minister she married my wife and I and when that marriage didn't work out, we walked and talked about what happened and what didn't happen in that relationship. People with similar backgrounds can be very healing for us as they listen, sharing their experiences and the wisdom they gained from those situations. Not everybody will be able to do this, so it's best to be discerning about who you choose or who chooses you. Emma taught me to listen first, digest the words and feelings, then slowly respond with care, truth, and wisdom. I had released or transformed my old way of approaching situations, which was blurting out the first thing in my mind not my heart. My sponsor David called it being like a sawed-off shotgun where everybody got sprayed.

On those walks and talks, the ebb and flow of wisdom reshaped me, my heart, and my outer world. I would go on similar walks by myself, taking my sage, tobacco, and drum with me to offer those medicines as I walked, listened, and offered prayers for Great Spirit to change my broken heart and give me the tools to become and remain whole.

When I traveled back and forth to Sedona before eventually moving there, I continued my practice of walking and communing with the earth. I would go out in the middle of the day, walk to a certain point, sit, take off my shoes, prepare my drum by smudging it, smoke the pipe, and offer tobacco to earth and spirits. I drummed and through the drum and in the air of my surroundings, songs would flood into my mind, heart, and out through my mouth. I usually recorded them on my phone to retain them.

The songs came in languages not familiar to my ear. I repeated and repeated them until I sang them from memory and as I sang them from my heart, I sang them from mammary. I called it this because of the drum. The sound of the drum spoke from the first place I heard it, which was as I grew inside of my mother. I held the memories of her heartbeat as I fed from her mammaries. This came to me as I was sitting on the iconic Bell Rock in Sedona, not far from where I lived. This was the place people and tourists usually stopped to take in their first glimpses of the red rocks. To me, this was a place to feed from. I didn't view it as a bell, I experienced it as a nipple and areola of Mother Earth as she fed and nourished me with the songs and the teachings I was given when I sat, drummed, and honored her.

I would walk and sit in the hundred plus degree heat of summer in the middle of the day - which wasn't very wise as the Arizona desert can be harsh. I would wear only a large straw hat from Ghana, Africa as it would cover my face and shoulders as I walked shirtless to feel Grandfather Sun on my skin. My walks were usually about two miles long and I would seek out places where I couldn't be seen so I wouldn't be distracted by the many tourists around. I would climb up on Courthouse Butte and seek out shallow caves behind juniper trees to sit, make my offerings, drum, and sing.

In those shallow caves I couldn't be seen from the trails below and could make my offerings without being disturbed. I will add that just because I couldn't be seen didn't mean I couldn't be heard. My songs filled the air from behind the Juniper trees and could probably be heard for hundreds of yards by many, but I still remained undisturbed.

The more I walked and connected to Mother Earth, the more I was given songs to sing for my evolution and self-healing. I believe they were medicine songs given to me for just this purpose. After receiving the songs, I continued to sing them over and over again. I also began to sing them in my ceremonies. Before, I only knew one traditional song, the first and only song I learned in ceremonial lodge, which was from the Chumash people of the California central coast near Santa Barbara and Santa Ynez.

One day as I sat with my elders and the other men, we were asked if anybody had a song or songs to sing, which nobody responded to. I stepped out of my fear and said that I did. I began to drum and sing, with all the men enthusiastically joining in with their voices and drums. I was asked if I had any more. My happy heart said yes and all the songs I sang were well received.

I only sing these songs for ceremonies, to welcome people to events I am involved in, or as I begin healing sessions. When I give a talk, I open and close with a song and if the spirits ask me to, I sing when they request it. I shared a lot of my healing work on social media and when I did, I began to sing the appropriate song or songs for the healing of those listening and watching. Some let me know they had begun singing those songs when they were in nature connecting to their higher self. They would say that they didn't know if they were singing them right - and I would reply that there is no right or wrong way to sing these songs, only the willingness to sing them. This made me proud and gave me joy that I was able to offer these songs not only to myself, but to the world as a whole.

There are daughters, sons, uncles, aunties, grandmothers, grandfathers, friends, and neighbors that tell me their littles ones hear me singing through their phones or computers and the children are transfixed, singing with me when I am online. My heart has learned to soak in these words and feelings that I'm able to give to those at any age. I often laugh at myself as I never think others are listening, but they are and I remain grateful for the words and encouragement of others.

I've spent a lot of time walking alone in the Sedona wilderness, where I can listen best without distractions. It is a simple act of willingness to walk and listen to what first appears as silence but holds a quiet magic unique to this place. But like anywhere else, distractions are always just around the corner. I had to teach myself to maintain my focus without distraction.

When I arrive at a turnaround point to make my way back home, I always stop to sit and feel the ancestors in the mountains and rocks, again offering tobacco and burning sage as offerings. If nobody is around, I sing a song or two sometimes using a rattle. I look for the ancestors to show themselves as owls, hawks, and different kinds of animals. I even see spirits standing as sentinels over the land and see the trees, plants, and rocks the same way.

I don't believe I was brought to Sedona to only walk and listen, but these are my mainline connections, not just to the land, but to my inner self. It serves as an example to those who have been disconnected for a lifetime. Never being connected to the land and spirit, I didn't know that I didn't know. There were days I was overwhelmed by everything around me as I spent more and more time plugging in and creating my initial connection with source. In California, I spent time hiking in canyons where oil drilling had at one time been prominent. I'd spend hours walking, sitting on the earth within the chaparral, drumming and singing, making offerings, walking in places that I felt wanted to keep me out due to the difficulty of the path.

Or was I trying to create a path where there was no path? I would walk through areas and almost force my way through areas of thick reeds that I believe were once grass but had grown into thick reeds due to their placement in the canyon where water ran through. One day while walking, I struggled making my way through and kept falling down. By the time I reached the other side of the canyon I was exhausted and scraped up from the reeds.

The experience taught me that, like life itself, times might be difficult and not without struggle, but I could make it through based on the choices I make. This truth carried through my journey of change and transformation. I remained steadfast and true to myself and to those around me, both seen and unseen, regardless of what the road ahead appears to hold.

"Allowing myself to venture through the unknown
was the adventure of transformation."
~ Walking Crow

Chapter 11: The Elemental Breath

Moving through life, I never considered breathing as an option for healing or how it even affected my body on a daily basis. I mean, it's just breathing, isn't it? Even living with undiagnosed asthma, I couldn't imagine that the burning in my lungs was not normal or different from anybody else. Everybody felt this, right?

Wrong!

Over the years of breaking cycles and freeing myself from the bondage of others' beliefs, I realized that the burning in my lungs was mirroring the burning in my unloved heart. I just didn't know how to correlate the feeling with the physical aspects of my experiences. I didn't have experiences like others. How could I or would I know what their experiences were? We didn't talk about things like that as children. If there were abuses, whether emotional, physical, or otherwise, they were unseen and unspoken. Mine were outwardly apparent and showed themselves through my anger, denial, and extreme loneliness.

During my time of transformation, I came to understand that I did not - and do not - need to convince anyone that I am innocent or prove that I am right about anything. It didn't matter whether others were listening when I was being interviewed, sharing, or teaching on my own about healing.

The radio and television shows I produced with Tiffany White Sage Woman didn't track listener or viewer numbers, so I never knew whether anyone was tuning in. But during that period, I realized the shows weren't really for others. They existed so that both little Anthony and big Anthony could hear their own voices, to witness and understand the journey of two individuals coming together as the whole, with his own understanding, love, and care for himself. I accepted myself exactly as I was and I am.

It wasn't for others, a truth I came to understand as I spoke week after week. This was my passageway into complete listening, both to the spoken words and the silence behind them. Understanding the healing medicine held in the silence between words allowed me to just sit and be.

Breaking family cycles wasn't something I talked about much, if at all. My focus was on my behavioral patterns and breaking old cycles, not to place blame, but simply to understand the when and why of the broken child and where it all began. As I sat in the silence between words, I followed my breath as it moved through my lungs landing in the place of my inner fire. That fire was stoked by gentle acceptance. With each breath, my lungs expanded after a lifetime of not giving myself proper breath or even knowing what that meant.

My body's inability to breathe properly in the womb and as a young child came from my father's abuse while my fragile body grew within my mother, where I should have been safe. Should have? In the house of an alcoholic there is no safety. It's just a matter of time before the explosion happens, and it always happens. This is the way it was in the womb and as I grew up in that house.

I can't imagine it was any easier for my father in the house or houses he grew up in. I mean his alcoholism came from somewhere and the tough life he had growing up. Understand, I'm not making excuses for him, but I was the one breaking the chain and healing my ancestry. Forgiveness and understanding were offered as I have offered it to myself. This isn't just for my dad, but for my mom as well.

The cycle of alcoholism was an important one. I swore I would never be like my father, yet I got in line right behind him and followed suit. This wasn't intentional on my part; it is just where life took me as I made bad decisions for myself. Dad and I would have arguments about his drinking because I was tired of it. But who was I to throw stones?

I don't believe I would have been able to make better decisions for myself at the time. The cycles of lineage are not easy to break as most times we can't see what's hiding in plain sight and even when we're looking in the mirror, staring into our own face, the truth is denied.

Not only was asthma a part of the damage I carried in my body, but along with that came migraine headaches that actually landed me in bed or the emergency room. The migraines started in my late twenties a couple of years before the end of my drinking. I remember teaching a class at the dance studio and I could barely make it through the class. By the time it ended, I was in incredible pain. I was vomiting and had diarrhea at the same time, which was such a terrible experience. When my body emptied out, a friend had to drive me home and put me to bed. Situations like this continued for years, even into my first marriage.

I began to track my food because of a migraine experience I had with my first wife and mother at a sober Christmas party. I got sick at the party even though we hadn't been there for more than half an hour. I had eaten a piece of cheese and a chocolate truffle with cocoa sprinkled on top and drank a cup of Diet Coke. That seems to have been enough to trigger the migraine. Mom and my wife Kimberly had to carry me to the car and drive me home to put me to bed. They placed a damp cloth over my eyes and I slept until the next day, waking up exhausted from the experience.

I remember having a migraine years before and I had to drive myself home at night in the rainstorm. When I finally made it home, I vomited and put myself in bed until I woke up the next day. I remembered what I ate at one point in the day before the episode. I had eaten a brownie pastry with cocoa sprinkled on top and drank a bottle of Diet Coke. This was the start of tracking my food. I realized the episodes were caused by the combination of aspartame in the Diet Coke and the sulfites in cheese combined with the cocoa was triggering a chemical reaction that was poison to my system.

Even after we moved to Tennessee the episodes continued, sometimes landing me in the hospital. All this time I thought I was suffering from food poisoning. When I saw the doctor, he asked whether I had vomited. When I answered yes, it was then he diagnosed me with migraine headaches. All through those years, I had believed it was food poisoning. In all honesty, I was poisoning myself without realizing it, giving myself poisons because I didn't know how to give myself better things out of ignorance and not understanding my emotional body. I chose poor relationships and poor foods, giving myself an unhealthy lifestyle.

I began to realize that I was choosing relationships where I was not really receiving. Just because someone expresses love doesn't mean it is real. There are those who use the word love to offer assurance where there is none. I went out of my way to give and do for others but rarely was there reciprocity. I was a people pleaser and didn't know how to give and do things for the right reasons. I wanted to be loved without having to ask for it and being a people pleaser was and is a form of begging.

In my nine-year marriage, I was usually given a couple of pairs of socks or underwear for Christmas. On my birthday, my then-wife would always ask, "What is your mother doing for your birthday?" She never offered to celebrate that particular day on her own. How would I know what my mother was thinking? I understand this clear as day. Love offers. Love gives. Love doesn't keep score. But when two people who are needy and don't know how to offer love for love's sake, it becomes a tragedy. Over time, I became weary and knew I had to leave that marriage.

During those years, I carried the burden of sinus issues, allergies, asthma, and the diagnosis of diabetes. I was a sick man in a sick relationship, and it became more than glaringly obvious. Years later, after becoming a healer, I understood where those issues lived in my tissues. They came from a lifetime of not feeling loved, having low or no self-esteem, and holding deep anger. All of that had been festering and incubating in my body until it was time to show itself. The issues in my tissues is something I became familiar with and talk about openly.

I understood the sinus and allergy issues stemmed from the stuck mucus in my nasal cavity after living with a broken heart and esteem issues for so many years. I took sinus meds and carried an inhaler for years. One day as I worked in the rose garden surrounding my house, I decided to stop taking any sinus meds and began slowing down the use of the inhaler. I began to limit the synthetic chemicals I was giving myself after believing they would make me healthier. They didn't, my marriage didn't, and my broken heart didn't. All the issues and symptoms came from one place, and it was time to learn how to be happy within my own life, instead of trying to make others happy and bypassing my own life and heart in the process.

One day I talked openly with my wife, expressing that I wasn't happy and didn't want to be married anymore. I had previously spoken to her about where we lived and said that I wanted to move. We were caretakers of a church in Studio City, California and had lived there rent free for eight years. We had no savings, weren't getting any better off financially, she wouldn't find a job to help us, and the responsibility of the property and my other employment fell mostly on my shoulders. I was tired. She proclaimed, "If we move, we'll have to pay rent." I responded with yes, what's wrong with that? She refused to make a change. That's when I knew it was time to leave that marriage and take care of myself. I understood I was in this alone and didn't need a spouse to feel more alone than I already felt.

I eventually moved and filed for divorce. I didn't know it at the time, but that decision opened the door to my healing journey. All I had to do was say *YES* and step through. It became a journey of opening my heart and giving myself what I believed should be simple…love!

I was given the opportunity to manage a sober living facility which offered rent free living and no salary. It was a temporary situation that proved challenging. I kept my sales job as I pursued self-healing and learning more about walking the Red Road. Typical of a person who is needy, I started seeing someone I met on social media. It very quickly turned into a sexual relationship. Not the smartest thing, but at the time I was still chasing a quick fix - despite my sobriety. The relationship wasn't a quick fix, but still dangerous for my wellbeing. We had lunch one day and she asked what I would do if she cheated on me. Really, this is how it starts? I got up from the booth, turned to face away from her, and said, "See this, this is the back of my head. It's the last thing you will see of me." That conversation or any kind like it was never had again.

I remember the words of my AA sponsor, *"Two ding-a-lings don't make a bell."* It made me laugh hysterically, but I never really thought about it. Here I was again, doing the same thing expecting a different result. The lady in that relationship actually treated me differently, she planned and celebrated me with a 50-year birthday party. Even though I was involved in planning and putting it together, it was something I wasn't used to. The day came for the party and some friends and family showed up. Most didn't due to the torrential rains we were having at the time. My mother came, but she was angry at me because of the divorce. She wasn't so nice to me or my new partner. Time passed, and I had my first healing experience, which is when I decided to follow that path and found a healing arts school to attend.

The relationship with this partner lasted almost two years. In time her abusive ways took a toll on my healing heart. I decided to leave and never return.

As I spent time working with others and healing my heart, my breathing became less labored, and I no longer used the inhaler I had carried for six years. The inhaler had expired, but I carried it anyway just in case I had an asthma episode. Those became fewer and fewer and the same with my sinus issues, the more I cared for my inner child and merged him with the man. I stopped using all those external synthetic chemicals. My heart, lungs, and breathing became stronger and deeper. The merging came as I recognized old wounds and forgave myself for carrying those burdens.

Most people don't understand how important forgiveness is. They assume forgiveness is something you offer others, but when healing your emotional body, forgiving yourself comes first. From there, forgiving others becomes easier and clearer. Learning to look within with an open heart and clear vision was the magic that transformed me. And that transformation became my primary purpose. As I like to say, *"Let go, let good. Let go, let God."*

I found that I didn't have to have a specific version of God or a particular cultural meaning of a god. Whatever I chose was fine and I no longer had to fight or argue with anyone about it, which gave me an internal feeling of peace.

As I slowed down and pulled myself out of the rat race of the monkey mind I was living in, I took time to sit during my walks and hikes to meditate or have a song and prayer ceremony. When I had my drum with me to do song and prayer ceremony, I would sit in the middle of a grassy area. My mindfulness through singing and drumming would slow me down even more. The rest of the world was passing by just feet or yards away, but the peace I experienced was solely mine and no one ever bothered or interrupted me. When I finished, I would carefully pack my drum and medicine bag. I often noticed the local Crows left feathers, even if they weren't meant for me. I told myself they were meant as gifts for me and I would gather them in my medicine bag. Sometimes those who heard the singing and drumming from a distance would thank me or greet me with gracious smiles as I made my way to my car.

I understand that the short ceremonies I created weren't just for me, but for all people, even those rushing by in their cars who were unaware of my presence. I knew I was there, and I understood perfectly that what I was doing not only had a profound effect on me, but on the world around me. The medicine of ceremony and spirit was and is powerful and through it I began to inner-stand the power of what I once believed I was offering only to myself.

Birthing, then playing the drums and singing the songs I was given had a profound effect on those that listened. After presenting them on social media, I received messages from all around the world expressing joy and love for the songs I was singing. They told me how their children and grandchildren would light up and run to where they could hear me and see me on the computer screen or smart phone. Not having children of my own but understanding my child within, my heart expanded hearing and reading these messages from moms, grandmothers and others who enjoyed my offerings.

I also held drum journey circles where I smudged, sang, prayed, and then drummed for twenty to twenty-five minutes, sending those in attendance into a deep and profound journey to the lower world to interact with their spirit guides, spirit animals, and ancestors in the place of the fire. As the drumming came to an end, I would bring them back into their bodies and into the room from wherever they had journeyed to. When they had returned and were fully present, I opened up the room for sharing of their journeys and powerful experiences.

It became apparent that my pattern of making poor decisions wasn't over when I entered into a new romantic relationship - the last I would have for years. She, too, was a healer coming into her way of being. We got along great, but as the saying goes, when there are *issues in the tissues*, they eventually rise to the surface and show where work still needs to be done.

I carried a deep belief that I was never enough when in romantic relationships. I was enough to begin with, enough to get involved with, but not enough to stay with, work through challenges, or build a better relationship with. That kind of commitment always seemed like too much trouble and moving on became the typical answer.

I tried not to become consumed with feelings of failure, anger, hurt, and sadness when I realized I didn't have the ability to be in a relationship. Not yet, anyway. I knew that because of my relationship with my mother. I needed to create a loving connection with her - without expecting anything in return. I had to allow myself to just love her, without waiting for a return on my investment.

This was the beginning of repairing the cracks and breaks in my heart that I had suffered with for a lifetime. The longer I stayed out of romantic relationships, the closer my mom and I became. The mother wound was the mother lode, lol. I had my work cut out for me. I never talked to my mom about healing our relationship. I mean, I know the issue was mine. All I really had to do was show up, allow her to be herself without judgement or expectation, not ask for anything, and bring as much love and presence into her world as possible. And something amazing happened. It began to work and I didn't have to work it. Our relationship softened, becoming warm and fuzzy. Over time, mom has said things to me I never imagined or expected.

I had this old belief that I should have been loved just because I was her son. My misguided beliefs kept me angry for what seemed like a lifetime. Through years of self-healing and deep forgiveness, I was able to release the anger, the shoulds, have-tos, and neediness I carried that told me she *had* to love me. I believe there are no have-tos in life and had to accept that. Once during a visit with Mom, I was sitting with her making small talk, as we always did. At one point, she stopped, looked at me, and said, "You are a good boy and I am proud of you."

WHAT???

I don't know what kind of look I had on my face, but my insides were on fire with gratitude and happiness. I can't believe I didn't explode or have fireworks shoot out of the top of my head. I was a sixty-three-year-old man and those words had never been spoken to me in my life. I was beside myself with joy, as happy as anybody could be. I tried not to show my exuberance about what I had just heard but graciously thanked her and simmered in a joy I had never known.

Mom and I had grown closer over the years of my transformation and breaking of unhealthy cycles. You should know the results of deep shadow work do not show themselves overnight and as I did the shadow work, I didn't expect immediate results. But when I noticed changes in the way I was becoming in the world, I became proud of the little boy and the man who had been estranged from each other as they merged in love. I believe mom saw and experienced my transformation simply by my presence.

I truly believe, as a younger person who felt unloved, my choice was "Heart, lungs, air, I don't have the capacity to love, I don't have the (lung) capacity to be loved." I didn't grovel or beg for love from others, I turned inwards and began loving myself the way I always wanted to be loved. I chose things for my life that were kinder, healthier, and more truthful. Inhaling the winds of truth never felt so good - without the burning in my lungs as it once had. A quote I repeated over and over to myself was - and still is "Heart, lungs, air - I love. I'm loved. Heart, lungs, air - I have the capacity to love, I have the (lung) capacity to be loved."

Presence is the ribbon that shows itself through connection.
~ Walking Crow

Chapter 12: The Ultimate Trust, Contentment of the Rooted Tree

"I am the tree that wasn't knocked down by the four winds, there are thousands of them (winds)." What are yours?
"I am rooted and I am fruited and I extend my branches to the heavens and the birds of the air rest in my branches and eat of my fruit. And what is my fruit? My fruit is simply the experience that I share of how I got from point A to point B. That's it and that's all."

These are what I call "crowisms" that I was given at the beginning of my walk down the path of the Red Road toward my new way of being. The words came to symbolize the transformation that was taking place in my life and how important it was. I understood because what I was experiencing was so powerful I had to share it with whomever would listen. So I did!

As the blessings of what I call "crowisms" came to me in my stillness, I knew I had to share them. They came from a place so deep and so far away, I was unsure if anybody would listen – especially coming from a guy like me. I say a guy like me because I didn't yet believe that I had anything to offer to anybody. But as I moved through my life and shared my experiences, those with interest began to show themselves, giving me hope. They shared love with me because of my words. I was invited to stay with families in their homes, and they'd introduce me to their neighbors and friends. Imagine the honor I felt sitting at the tables and sleeping in the warm comfortable beds of people that were no longer strangers. I learned about their spouses and children and the lives they had lived. We became sisters and brothers…Soul families!

I began to realize that I was poking the bear and my words had more impact than I could fathom. They were profound and thought provoking. They not only provoked thought, but they stirred hearts and feelings, which was really my intention.
A sister who lives nearby asked what I was trying to say because she didn't understand it. I answered that I was here to "poke the bear,"

and that what I had to say wasn't for everybody. She asked if I was a provocateur and I responded, "That is exactly what I am!"

Saying that, I accepted my role and stood up straight and strong in my position as a tree that is "rooted and fruited." Understanding my accepted role, I became fearless and never again worried about critics and backlash. I trusted my words and I trusted myself and the spirit world that gave me the specific quotes, saying, limericks, and questions I posed to the general public. More and more I gained favor with people searching for change, acceptance, truth, love, and understanding. I pushed my proverbial finger into their chest with my words and stirred the pot. This allowed them to question themselves and the life they were living and lived.

Mind you, I am no Guru, Master, or Master teacher, but there is much to say and it comes from the deep shadow work I have done over the years and continue to do. I simply share my insights with the world. Having the bravery to use my voice and words, I became a vehicle for deeper healing by mentoring others to change their thoughts, words, and the ways they did or didn't treat themselves. It was like giving them permission for the first time in their lives to think, feel, and be outside the box on their own terms. I understand that box completely. I was forced to live within the parameters of a box by well-meaning parents and a society that really didn't promote individuality or freedom of self-expression. "Sit down, stand up, be quiet, raise your hand, get in line, get a job. Be quiet, be quiet, be quiet!"

These are the messages I received in my early life. I obviously wasn't alone as I learned from those who were reacting to my words of hope and the questions that poked and stirred the bear. Many of the teachings from spirit I repeated to myself over and over again. I began to post them on social media with a picture of myself as I transcended my journey and the old life that seemed to be melting away. Alchemy was my destination, a place of transformation, transcendence, transition, and transmutation. I am the gold I sought, and I was the gold within.

Along the way people have asked, "What does your name Walking Crow mean?" I explain, "Crow medicine is the keeper of the sacred law, it is alchemy, shapeshifting, moving from darkness to light, darkness to light, darkness to light." The last part of my statement I always repeat three times as the number three is the number of springtime, new beginnings, the planting of new seeds and sunrise in the medicine wheel in the direction of the east. This is a powerful statement of acceptance of my place as Walking Crow, the embodiment of Transformational Sacred Drum Medicine, and the four elements of earth, water, fire, and air and how I have become willing to live and learn and be the alchemist incarnate.

Living as the embodiment of the Walking Crow and understanding my elemental journey allowed me to understand duality and that I was both spirit and earth. When folks again ask, "Why Walking Crow?" I simply explain how I walk on earth and live in the heavens as well.

My friend Angela didn't know who I was. We met on social media, after she heard me talk about living in the duality of my left side being the divine feminine and my right side being the divine masculine. She said she had never heard a man talk that way. Surprised, I replied "Well, you have now," and over the years we became friends. She and very few others witnessed my full journey of transformation in real time. She is a witness and a supporter of who and what I have become, trudging through the aspects of change that were not so easy or comfortable. She has been one of the biggest parts of my journey. Although as friends do or don't always agree or agree to disagree, we have been tethered by the spirit world and our individual spiritual beliefs. When the words "Can I get a witness?' are uttered in churches, the reply is always "Amen!"

I spoke those very words and witnesses have been with me throughout my journey. Many have moved along on their separate paths, but those who say yes to me are with me in relationship, nurturing the nature of love and true friendship. This is notable to me, as growing up there we didn't have best or close friends. When my tribe from grade school went on without me, I never even questioned my loneliness or the why of it. It wasn't until I was an adult that I understood how I was affected by the lack of companionship and friendship. The shadow work I did revealed my deep loneliness, but walking the path of the Red Road I began to inner-stand that I was never alone. Loneliness came from the external world, and I was steeped in self-awareness. I discovered how to go within and find peace in the stillness and darkness of my own quiet beauty.

Finding peace and ease became primary as I walked the path of the curandero/healer. Playing the drums and using rattles as part of my ritual practice takes me to other worlds of spirits, spirit animals, and the understanding of how to walk forward seemingly alone, but never without the guidance of the spirit world.

My father, who passed over thirty years ago, showed himself from time to time to show loneliness had no validity. Grandma Carmen's mom's mom walked with me as well. This made me happy and felt good; when she was alive I didn't feel she liked me very much. Or maybe, like my mother, I didn't let her get close enough to be able to accept her for her.

I have a spirit guide named Mogly that showed himself early in my healing practice and he's been with me ever since. He is a tall seven to eight foot being who looks like he is made of stone. He wears a loincloth, other times he's seen wearing a Buckskin suit with a beautiful war bonnet. He is very impressive and ominous looking. When he first came to me or when I first saw him, he looked like the "Jungle Book" character whose name is actually "Mowgli." I saw him when I had my hand on a fellow student during a spirit guide exercise in our training for energy healing. I had my eyes closed but could see "Mowgli" swimming through my arm, that looked to be filled with blue, blue water. He was swimming like a fish. The next time I saw him, I didn't actually see him, I felt him. He was a powerful spirit.

I believe he shows himself as stone to teach me the power of grounding and what being grounded can offer if I'm willing to understand, rather than getting caught up in the parroting of others and their inability to get grounded and remain grounded. In this form Mogly represents the Earth itself and what it takes to be a powerful being in this universe.

I've always experienced him as expressionless, his facial features barely recognizable, but notable. His communication with me is silent, allowing me to understand what it is to hear, feel, and know through silence and telepathy. At other times, he appears as "Two Feathers," usually when I am receiving a healing or journeying. Two Feathers is a powerful, stately presence that oversees what I am doing and how I move through the world. He is always seen with his arms crossed, wearing Buckskin, with long silver hair partially tied back like mine, adorned with two eagle feathers. He gazes into the distance and never speaks. He simply sits, observing and taking everything in, always visible to me during significant moments, like the healings I receive.

I believe Two Feathers is Mogly shapeshifting into a different version of himself. I also believe - and it has been communicated to me - that I am also Two Feathers and that the name Two Feathers is another name I carry. I haven't talked about that much. For over three years, I have come to more than understand who and what I am. I have been shown that I am an ancient being and as old as time, which explains the knowledge and understandings I carry and share with others. I believe that Mogly may be the oldest version of me as he is shown to me as stone.

Earlier I mentioned how I first saw Mogly as "Mowgli." Showing Mowgli to me as he was a child was actually showing me the boy I originally was. My misunderstanding of his name was purposeful, as my name wasn't as important as my *being*. During the writing of this book the correct version of the name was shown to me. I understood the name to be Mogly, so I stayed with it. I didn't get angry or feel dumb or think anything more than "Okay," and moved on. So Mogly it is, lol!

My intention in expressing who and what I am is to offer you the possibility of accepting the simple truth of who you are and where you come from. I've spent most of this lifetime trying to be what somebody else was and to have what I thought they had. The plain truth is they are not me and I am not them.

I had to learn and understand the true portals of intake into my being sit eighteen inches above my heart, while the intake of my eyes, ears, nose, and mouth continuously receive and are bombarded with false information rooted in materialism. That noise kept me in my head, running on the squeaky wheel of self-doubt, anger, hate, uncertainty and feeling unloved. The noise of distractions is so loud and overpowering that we grow confused about what to do. We make choices that would be far simpler and much easier if we only listen with our heart instead of filtering endless misinformation and distraction.

In the early days of my new walk, I often talked about how I lived on a squeaky wheel and how the noise of that wheel drowned out my heart, how I couldn't hear my own my heartbeat. As clarity came, I began to hear the gentle voice of spirit, patient and caring. At times there was no voice or sound at all, only the feeling of safety, of being held, like that place I had traveled so far from, that place within my mother where I first felt that presence. It was the sound and feeling I had been receiving from Mogly and Two Feathers for years, a place of being held in the arms of mother father god and in the ancient way of earth, water, fire, and air.

Stone Mogly showed me how to be grounded with my roots running deep into the earth, my ancient tree branches reaching high into the sky, standing as a pillar in a massive forest of life-giving trees. I was rooted and fruited and finally inner-stood my place on this earth, extending my branches for all to see. In the forest, I inner-stood I was part of the whole and as the tree, my place was right where I was standing.

Patience was no longer the issue nor, was being silenced. I had come into my voice and spoke from a place of love. My voice became the sound of wind whistling through my branches as I swayed alongside the others. In that gentleness, I found peace in my abilities and the gentle rhythms that move me.

As I grew, the peace in me grew as well and I began to inner-stand how the *piece* inside me was growing simultaneously, getting bigger and stronger. I was given a mantra to support my growth and I began to share it with others. I placed stones of different sizes on my desk. As I repeated the mantra, I would pick up a stone, hold it in my hand, then set it down and choose a larger one. As I proceeded through the stones, I spoke to the growing peace/piece within me.

The Peace/Piece in Me

The peace in me is the piece in me and the piece in me is the peace in me
The piece in me is the peace in me and the peace in me is the piece in me
The peace in me is the piece in me and the piece in me is the peace in me
The piece in me is the peace in me and the peace in me is the piece in me

~ Walking Crow

The beauty of finding my peace was - and still is - knowing that I am not alone. The spirit world walks with me, or I should say, I walk with it, as it guides me through difficult, tough times. They show themselves proudly as I make my way through small triumphs and great leaps along my journey. I honor them by recognizing their presence, speaking their names, and sharing their messages with others, who may or may not be struggling.

One of the things that became clear as I continually said *YES* to my journey was that I became the fruited tree that I talked about for years. Outside my home there is a Grandmother Pine tree that represents all grandmother trees. When I see her, I offer tobacco, smudge, and thanks for the breath of life she gives me. Those of us on the Red Road refer to grandmother trees as the standing nations.

I told myself years ago when I said *YES* to my path that I wanted to learn to be selfless like the grandmother trees, after a lifetime of selfishness. The trees came to represent much of my new life. As I grow within the forest, I know how my roots grow deep into the earth and are interconnected with other trees, building a strong community foundation. At the same time my branches reach high into the heavens, crossing and entwining themselves with the branches of neighboring trees, creating an even stronger and cohesive bond of community.

Through the examples of the grandmothers, I have learned selflessness and released the selfishness of the child. My hope for those who suffer in humanity is they (you) will be willing to look around and within for examples of what is ready to be released, and how healing can be internalized. By loving ourselves enough, we become the tree – rooted and fruited - inviting others to say *YES* to their own life.

When no one was willing to say yes to me, it was I that became willing to give the breath of life to myself with a simple, but meaningful *YES*, after a lifetime of no.

Know that you are not alone. As the tree, you stand on your own in your power, but in the forest, you stand in your power with the strength of community, love, friendship, and understanding.

Will you say *YES* to yourself after a lifetime of no?

Say *YES* to yourself. You owe nobody anything but yourself…*YES*!

In the early days of my walk, when I woke up in the morning before doing anything else, I placed my feet on the floor and allowed myself to connect deep into Mother Earth, inviting her energy to rise up through my legs. Once I was plugged in, I opened my pineal gland to allow the heavens and universal qi/energy to flow through the crown of my head, down my spine, and snake its way through my body to meet the energy rising from Mother Earth. Once I was filled or fulfilled, I would quietly sit in the feeling of wholeness and fullness.

How will you start your days? What will you give yourself first? How will you begin your new life?

I choose not to give these writings an ending, because this path does not end. Like roots still reaching and branches still growing, the walk continues. What I have shared is not a conclusion, but a doorway.

This… this is only the beginning.

Love and Blessings,
~ Walking Crow

About the Author

Anthony J Rodriguez was born February 24, 1961, in San Fernando, California and began his life living in the nearby suburb of Pacoima. As a young man battling drug addictions and alcoholism, he was arrested for driving drunk and found himself sober, beginning a new life. After being married and divorced several times, Anthony received an energy healing from a friend, and the experience changed his life. He moved in a direction he didn't even know was possible. It set him on a new path of transformation and change. Because of that healing session, he decided to become an energy healer and found a school that would teach him how.

As he began transforming his life, he found the Red Road and the indigenous teachings of the natives of Turtle Island (the Americas). Anthony eventually developed his own way of healing called Transformational Sacred Drum Medicine. Many teachers appeared, but most important to him was Rev. Emma Molina-Ynequez, who eventually named him Walking Crow.

Walking Crow has helped others from all over the world, offering healing sessions, mentoring, ceremony, teaching, working with the emotional body, making drums and rattles and being a hollow bone continuing to transform and help others to do the same.

> *"I have transformed from a seemingly hopeless state of mind and body.*
> *I was never hopeless, I was only helpless.*
> *I asked for help and I remain hopeful."*

~ Walking Crow
Transformational Sacred Drum Medicine
Sedona, Arizona

More Offerings from Walking Crow

Walking Crow is a Transformational Shamanic Healer, Curandero, Mentor, Medicine Man, Drum and Rattle Maker, Ceremonialist, Seer, Storyteller, Philosopher, Speaker, Published Author and Media Host. His emphasis is working with those who want to change and heal their lives. His private practice includes shamanic healing and mentoring sessions, personal and group drum journeys, healings, and clearing ceremonies. He also conducts workshops that teach others how to be in their bodies, change their language about speaking about who they are and are not, and how to come to peace with life's traumas, hurts, wounds, and shames using the chakra system, subtle energy of the emotional body, and the medicine wheel.

Walking Crow celebrates his ancient lineages including the Tarahumara and Purépecha through his mother and Chichimeca through his father. He has been guided by his ancestral spirits to birth (make) Sacred Drum Medicine and to sing the medicine songs he is given by the spirit world.

As a Shamanic drummer, Walking Crow helps others journey into other dimensions to find their spirit guides, spirit animals, gifts, healings or simply to find answers in an organic way. Walking Crow channels Drum Medicine, including rattles, tobacco, and other plant medicines. He has birthed drums for many all over the world and travels Turtle Island extensively to share his gifts. He hosts Sacred Drum Birthing Ceremonies for groups and individuals, taught in a ceremonial and intentional way. Medicine song singing circles, fire and full moon ceremonies are also available.

Walking Crow is also available for retreats and speaking engagements, private or corporate. Services and Sessions provided are available in person and remotely via Video Conference.

Transformational Shamanic Healing * Medicine Song Circles
Mentoring Men in Self Care * Talking Circles * Ceremonialist
Also available for purchase or by special order: Medicine Drums, Shamanic Rattles, Drum Mallets, and Ceremonial Blankets
www.sacreddrummedicine.com

www.ingramcontent.com/pod-product-compliance
Lightning Source LLC
Chambersburg PA
CBHW071759150726
47998CB00005B/1996